FALL HARVESTS

FALL HARVESTS

A Southern Seasons Book

Martha Phelps Stamps

A CUMBERLAND HOUSE HEARTHSIDE BOOK

Nashville, Tennessee

For my Daddy, Richard Phelps Stamps,
on his seventy-fifth birthday.

Published by Cumberland House Publishing, Inc.
431 Harding Industrial Drive, Nashville, Tennessee 37211

Design by Gore Studio, Inc., Nashville, Tennessee.
Photography by Meryl Truett.

Library of Congress Cataloging-in-Publication Data

Stamps, Martha
    Fall harvests : menus and recipes that celebrate autumn's bounty /
Martha Phelps Stamps ; photography by Meryl Truett.
        p. cm.
    "A Cumberland House hearthside book."
    Includes index.
    ISBN 1-58182-000-3 (pbk. : alk. paper)
    1. Cookery, American—Southern style. 2. Menus. 3. Autumn.
I. Title.
TX715.2.S68S78   1998
642'.4—dc21   98–36225
                                                          CIP

Printed in the United States of America
1 2 3 4 5 6 7 — 02 01 00 99 98

Contents

CONTENTS

OCTOBER

CONTENTS

NOVEMBER

CONTENTS

Introduction

Welcome to *The Southern Seasons*, a series of books that lives in and cooks with each particular season in a place called home. Local, seasonal food is important to me on a few levels. Eating in harmony with the rhythms of earth puts you that much closer to nature. God provides for us with beauty and bounty in each of the seasons. In recent decades, farming, groceries, and our very existence have become more regulated, more homogenous due to larger production and larger management. Most of us eat produce and farm stock that is shipped and trucked clear across the nation, either adding the enormous cost of air freight, or compromising the quality of product by picking too green or spraying with chemicals to sustain "freshness." The individual, the unique has been the victim. Whether it is the scuppernong grape, which everyone in these hills once gathered and is now nearly impossible to find; or the small farmer, who now gets paid to grow tobacco instead of wholesome, native food crops; or the dairies or small smoke houses, or graineries that closed down when the huge national ones shut them out. Buying locally supports your home's economy and ecology.

Eating and cooking with a local and seasonal sensibility is simply a treat. I love to scour the local farmers' market for gifts from the earth. My earth. The earth around here. Don't give me asparagus in October, or peaches at Christmas. Each season has its unique blessing, its own treats. And if you listen closely, your tummy (and your soul) are usually yearning for just what the earth is providing. Sweet potatoes, squash and pumpkin in the fall. Cabbage and turnips, hearty stews and starches come winter. In the spring I crave a tonic of fresh greens and wild things; and in the summer make it light, with lots of fresh fruit and simply cooked vegetables. *The Southern Seasons* celebrates the uniqueness of all of the times of the earth, with menus inspired by the bounty at hand.

FALL HARVESTS

FALL

The first days of fall are among the most anitcipated in the South. As August bears on, with the worst of the summer heat lingering on at the end, we yearn for a break in the air. When at last the evenings cool and a few showers loosen the dirt, our gardens catch a second wind and start bearing fruit and flower with a steady ease until that first frost, and all of its sudden change. That's when Daddy gathers his greens, the pumpkins fill the market, and hunters pull out their waders. Fall feels patriotic. Like sweaters on girls at football games. Like pilgrims and turkeys and Jimmy Stewart and Norman Rockwell. Fall is full of the promise of change, bright and hopeful. The very air differs; it lightens somewhat, filling your vision with clarity. The fallen leaves smell so good, you want to bury yourself in a great big pile (I frequently do). You spend more time outside than you have in recent weeks. You want to walk, you want to run through crackling woods, you want to sing loud, silly, songs and kiss behind the bleachers. For my part, I want to grill every last vegetable before the first frost, I want to cook mustard greens, beets, fennel and cabbage. Roast sweet potatoes, simmer stews, bake apple crisps and puddings. I want to do everything in my rush of adrenalin, Autumn winds euphoria. I never have managed to do everything to suit my autumn mood. This year, perhaps.

SEPTEMBER

September is an in-between month. We're doing fall-ish things like back to school, football games, and the wearing of brown, but the heat seldom breaks before the middle of the month. And then, such a relief. The air takes on a clarity—we can breathe again. Our tired flowers and vegetables catch a second wind, too, making September one of our most beautiful months. September is a great time at the farmer's market, too. Now is the season to eat every tomato you can find—pick the green ones, too. Take pleasure in shelling your lima beans and black and pink eyes; they won't be around for long. This is the month when my morning glories and moon flowers really shine, and I cherish every moment on the porch or lying in the once-more-cool grass, taking note of the earlier sundown and later dawn. Our spirits lift along with the heat. We take on new projects and ideas and share them with our friends, along with a morsel or two, across a patio table or picnic cloth.

I.

Daddy's Birthday

Daddy is the southern food guru. Mama's in charge of the baked things, the pretty things, the fancy stuff. But step aside and let Daddy fry your chicken and your corn, put your beans on to simmer and clean your turnip greens. Daddy does the country stuff. The no-frills food that warms the soul. No-one taught him. His mamma didn't like to cook. He has told me he used to watch a gentleman that worked for his grandparents cook, and he picked up a few things.

Daddy's birthday is the first family celebration of fall. He'd be thrilled if we had barbecue every year, but this year I told him that I wanted to cook all southern "stuff," but with my own approach. "You know, Daddy, with all of those things I learned in culinary school."

"Hmmph," was what I heard. Not that Daddy doesn't approve of my classical training. He just doesn't want it applied to *his* food.

"Trust me," was my sweet reply. I still don't think he trusted me, but he did eat all of his food.

The Menu

Potato & Scallion Biscuits with Country Ham

———————

Green Tomato Chutney

———————

Marinated and Grilled Chicken Breasts

———————

Mashed Lima Beans with Fresh Goat Cheese

———————

Hot Slaw

———————

Damson Plum Upside Down Cake

———————

Crystallized Ginger Ice Cream

Potato Scallion Biscuits

I was inspired to create these because of the popularity of the Sweet Potato Biscuits from my first book. They turned out great, very moist and savory. I like them with any chutney or marmalade.

MAKES ABOUT 18 BISCUITS

3	medium (12-ounce) Yukon Gold or russet potatoes
2	cups butter, melted
2	cups all-purpose flour
3	tablespoons baking powder
½	tablespoon baking soda
¾	teaspoon salt
1	teaspoon black pepper
⅔	cup buttermilk
4	scallions, sliced thinly

Preheat the oven to 375°. Grease a cookie sheet. Scrub the potatoes clean and place on the prepared cookie sheet. Bake in the skins about 45 minutes until very soft. Peel and mash with the butter while still warm.

Turn the oven up to 400°. Sift together the dry ingredients and mix into the potatoes. Add the buttermilk and scallions and combine. Don't over mix. The dough will be quite tacky. Pat the dough down to ½ inch on a floured board and cut out with a floured biscuit cutter. Place 1-inch apart on the cookie sheet. Alternately, you may drop dough by the tablespoonful onto the cookie sheet. Bake for 20 minutes until well browned. Serve warm with marmalade and country ham.

Green Tomato Chutney

There are lots of tomatoes growing in the mid south through most of October, but you always run the risk of an early frost. Pick them green and take advantage of a late crop.

MAKES ABOUT 9 PINTS

3	large green tomatoes, chopped
1	large yellow onion, chopped
2	Granny Smith apples, cored and chopped
3	cups golden raisins
1½	pounds light brown sugar
3	cups cider vinegar
2	tablespoons mustard seed
1	tablespoon whole cloves
2	teaspoon red pepper flakes
1½	tablespoons salt

Mix everything together in a large non-reactive saucepan. Slowly bring to a simmer, stirring. Simmer, stirring often, for 2 hours. Process in sterilized jars or keep covered in the refrigerator for several weeks.

Marinated and Grilled Chicken Breasts

These have so much flavor! Please, even if you are dieting, leave the skin on the breast while it is cooking. It adds flavor as well as protecting the meat from drying out.

SERVES 8

8	split chicken breasts with skin and bones
¼	cup olive oil
2	lemons
4	cloves garlic, finely minced
1	bunch parsley, roughly chopped
2	tablespoons fresh thyme leaves
1	bay leaf, broken into three or four pieces
½	teaspoon salt
½	teaspoon black pepper
¼	teaspoon cayenne

Remove the bones from the breasts, leaving the skin on. Place in a non-reactive bowl or Pyrex and pour the oil over. Zest the lemons and add the zest to the bowl. Cut the lemons in half and squeeze the juice into the bowl. Add the remaining ingredients and stir or toss to coat well. Use your fingers to push a bit of the marinade up under the skin. Marinate in the refrigerator for at least 2 hours or overnight. Remove from the refrigerator 1 hour before grilling.

Heat a grill to medium high heat. Use tongs to remove the chicken from the marinade and blot a little of the oil off onto paper towels. Place the chicken skin side down on the grill and cook for about 4 minutes. Turn the chicken and cook about 5 to 7 more minutes until done. Serve hot or room temperature (they make a great sandwich the next day!).

Mashed Lima Beans with Fresh Goat Cheese

Okay, Daddy was a little leery of these. And I'm sure he wouldn't want his precious limas this way every day, but he licked his plate clean. I used a wonderful extra soft goat cheese from Fromagerie Belle Chevre. It's hand-made by Liz Parnell just over the state line in northern Alabama. I love having the opportunity to buy from local folks.

SERVES 8

3	*pounds fresh limas*
2	*teaspoons salt*
1	*bay leaf*
½	*teaspoon white pepper*
8	*ounces fresh mild goat cheese*
4	*large basil leaves, cut in thin strips*

Cover the lima beans generously with water. Add the salt, pepper, and bay leaf. Bring to a boil, skimming off the scum. Turn the heat down to medium and cook until done, about 10 to 15 minutes. Drain the beans, discarding the bay leaf. Place the limas in a bowl and add the goat cheese. Mash with a fork or potato masher, not too fine. Some beans may remain whole. Taste for seasoning and adjust with salt and pepper. Turn the oven to broil. Place the mashed limas in a baking dish and place under the broiler to lightly brown the top before serving. Garnish with basil leaves.

Hot Slaw

This is a beautiful dish, nice and vinegar-y and extra fresh tasting because of the herbs.

SERVES 8

¼	cup olive oil
½	red onion, sliced thinly
½	red bell pepper, sliced thinly
½	green bell pepper, sliced thinly
1	carrot, cut in 2-inch sticks
½	head purple cabbage, sliced thinly
1	teaspoon dry mustard dissolved in 3 tablespoons red wine vinegar
2	teaspoons salt
¼	teaspoon red pepper flakes
2	tablespoons roughly chopped fresh basil
2	tablespoons roughly chopped fresh mint

Heat the oil in a large skillet. Add the onion and cook about 2 minutes, leaving the heat on high and shaking the skillet a bit. Add the peppers and carrot and cook 2 more minutes. Add the cabbage and shake to combine. Cover the pan and cook about 3 minutes. Remove the lid and add the mustard and vinegar, along with the salt and red pepper, tossing or stirring to combine. Taste and adjust the seasoning. Toss the basil and mint on top just before serving the slaw warm.

ide-Down Cake

s our local plum. You can find them in at the farmers' market starting in August through the first of September. This cake is a delight. Beautiful and delicious.

SERVES 8 TO 12

PLUM BOTTOM LAYER:
¼	cup unsalted butter
½	cup firmly packed dark brown sugar
2	tablespoons bourbon
10	plums, cut in half, pit removed
½	cup chopped pecans

CAKE LAYER:
½	cup unsalted butter
½	cup plus 2 tablespoons sugar
3	eggs
1½	teaspoons vanilla extract
1¼	cups cake flour
1	teaspoon baking powder
½	teaspoon baking soda
¼	teaspoon salt
½	cup buttermilk

Preheat the oven to 375°.

To make the bottom layer, place the butter, brown sugar and and bourbon in a deep 10-inch cast iron skillet heated to medium on top of the stove, and cook until the butter and sugar melt. Remove from the heat and spread the mixture evenly in the bottom of the skillet. Place the plum halves in the skillet cut side up, encircling the

rim of the skillet and making smaller circles toward the center. Scatter the pecan pieces over all.

To make the cake layer, cream the butter and sugar until lemon colored and fluffy. Beat in the eggs one at a time. Mix in the vanilla. Sift the dry ingredients and add them to the batter. Gently pour the batter over the fruit and nuts and bake in the center of the oven, about 40 minutes until the cake is risen and golden and a toothpick inserted in the center comes out clean. Let the cake sit for a few minutes, then invert onto a serving platter. If any fruit happens to stick in the pan, simply lift it out and set it back in place.

Crystallized Ginger Ice Cream

My family is nuts about homemade ice cream! Both of my sisters and my parents (me too!) have ice cream makers in a constant state of readiness. I'm also nuts about crystallized ginger. You can buy it quite affordably at Asian markets. I eat it like candy.

MAKES ABOUT 1½ QUARTS

4	ounces crystallized ginger
2	cups whole milk
4	large egg yolks
1	cup superfine sugar
2	cups heavy cream, chilled

Roughly chop the crystallized ginger and set aside. Pour the milk into a saucepan and heat to simmering. Remove the pan from the heat. Heat about two inches of water in the bottom of a double boiler to simmering. Off the heat, place the egg yolks and sugar in the top of the double boiler and whisk together until pale yellow. Slowly pour in the hot milk, whisking. Place the top of the double boiler over the simmering (not boiling) water. The upper pan should not touch the water. Cook the custard, stirring constantly, for 8 to 10 minutes until the custard thickens enough to coat the back of a wooden spoon. Remove from the heat and stir in the crystallized ginger. Stir in the cream. Refrigerate for at least thirty minutes or as long as overnight. Pour into an ice cream freezer and freeze according to the manufacturer's instructions.

2.

Lunch for Meryl

I met my friend Meryl when I moved back to Nashville several years ago. We were instant friends with many of the same interests, including food. Meryl is always up for trying any new restaurant, the more obscure the location, the better. It's kind of like enjoying yard sales. It definitely gets to be a habit. She and I have ventured into some pretty scary territory in the endless quest for perfect barbecue or mashed potatoes.

Meryl loves to entertain, as well. She and her husband John renovated two beautiful old houses in East Nashville, decorated them in their own fabulous, funky style and threw fabulously funky wild parties as well as more genteel lunches for the ladies. They kept telling me they were moving to Savannah, close to Meryl's native coastal South Carolina and home of some of the *best* southern food. I guess I wasn't listening well because I was certainly surprised with their absence, and a bit at loose ends.

Meryl invited me to Savannah with promises of the local specialty crab pie, to be served on her screened in porch after the worst of the heat had ended. I was so excited, I went ahead and worked out the whole menu!

The Menu

Marinated Fall Mushrooms

———

Crab Pie with Green Tomatoes and Parmesan Sesame Crust

———

Bitter Green Salad with Peanuts and Bacon

———

Dried Peach Vinaigrette

———

Warm Figs with Honeyed Yogurt

———

Benne Cookies

Marinated Fall Mushrooms

I love mushrooms in the fall. Their woodsy flavor and aroma seem perfectly suited to the change in the air. Any wild mushroom will do. I'm very fond of the organic shiitakes grown on oak logs at The Farm in Summertown, Tennessee.

SERVES 6

1	pound fresh button mushrooms
1	pound fresh wild mushrooms (shiitakes, porcinis, morel, oyster, etc.)
4	tablespoons olive oil
1	teaspoon salt
	Black pepper, to taste
2	tablespoons white wine vinegar
	Juice and zest of 1 lemon
1	tablespoon fresh tarragon, if available (use parsley or mint, if not)

Preheat the oven to 400°. Clean the mushrooms and spread on a baking sheet. Toss with the olive oil, salt and pepper. Roast the mushrooms for 10 minutes. Place immediately in a mixing bowl and toss with the vinegar, lemon juice, and zest. Let cool and toss in the tarragon. Adjust the seasoning and serve at room temperature.

Crab Pie with Green Tomatoes and Parmesan Sesame Crust

You won't find this exact recipe in old Savannah books. I have taken a few liberties with tradition. The tart green tomatoes balance the rich crab meat.

SERVES 6

CRUST:

1¼ cups all-purpose flour

½ teaspoon salt

2 tablespoons sesame seeds

2 tablespoons freshly grated Parmesan cheese

¼ cup butter, cut in small pieces

¼ cup shortening

2 to 3 tablespoons ice water

FILLING:

4 tablespoons butter

½ yellow onion, chopped fine

3 cloves garlic, minced

2 green tomatoes, cored and chopped

2 teaspoons salt, or to taste

1 teaspoon white pepper

3 tablespoons all-purpose flour

1 teaspoon fresh rosemary leaves

1 teaspoon fresh thyme leaves

1 cup heated chicken stock

1 cup heated milk

　Pinch ground nutmeg

1 pound jumbo lump crab meat, well picked over

1   egg
2   tablespoons milk

Stir together the flour, salt, Parmesan, and sesame seeds in a large mixing bowl. Add the butter and shortening, and mix in using either your fingertips or a pastry blender. Work until the mixture resembles cornmeal. A few larger pieces of fat is okay; don't overmix. Sprinkle the water over the mixture and quickly work in by hand or with a rubber spatula. Add additional water if necessary just to make the mixture hold together. It will look rather shaggy. Gather the dough into a ball and flatten into a disc. Wrap in plastic and refrigerate for 1 hour or up to 3 days. The dough may be frozen, as well (if frozen, thaw in the refrigerator before continuing).

Heat the butter in a deep skillet. Add the onion and cook about 4 minutes until wilted. Add the garlic, tomatoes, salt, pepper, rosemary, and thyme, and cook on high, briefly stirring or shaking the pan, for about 7 minutes or until most of the moisture from the tomatoes has cooked out. Stir in the flour and let cook for a few minutes, stirring. Whisk in the stock and then the milk, whisking constantly to avoid lumps. Add the nutmeg and bring to a boil. Reduce the heat and simmer for 10 minutes, stirring as needed. Mix in the crab. Taste and adjust the seasonings and allow the mixture to cool.

Place the crab mixture in a deep pie plate or baking dish. Roll out the dough on a floured surface into a circle larger than the pan. Roll the dough up onto the rolling pin, and then unroll over the pie. Gather up the sides and crimp with your fingers or the tines of a fork. Cut a few slashes in the crust to let the steam escape. Refrigerate for at least 30 minutes before baking.

Meanwhile, preheat the oven to 375° and mix the egg with the milk. Brush this over the crust. Bake for about 40 minutes until the crust is nicely browned and the interior is bubbling. Serve warm.

Bitter Green Salad with Peanuts and Bacon

Pork, peanuts, and peaches. This salad truly pays tribute to Georgia.

SERVES 6

½	pound bitter salad greens, such as chicory and endive
6	strips country style (thick cut) bacon
½	cup Dried Peach Vinaigrette (recipe follows)
½	cup roasted, salted peanuts

Clean the greens and tear or cut into bite size pieces. Spin dry and set aside. Cook the bacon, drain, and tear into pieces. Place the greens in a salad bowl. Toss with the vinaigrette. Garnish with the bacon and peanuts, and serve.

Marinated Grilled Quail or Dove

Wilted Mustard Greens

Sweet Potato Mash

Applesauce with Cranberries

Dried Peach Vinaigrette

Nice and peachy, but not too sweet.

MAKES ABOUT 1½ CUPS, ENOUGH FOR 8 TO 12 SALADS

⅓   cup cider vinegar

3   cloves

½   stick cinnamon

2   tablespoons honey

    Zest and juice of 1 lemon

2   ounces dried peaches

2   cloves garlic

½   teaspoon salt

¼   teaspoon freshly ground black pepper

¼   teaspoon red pepper flakes

⅓   cup olive oil

⅓   cup vegetable oil

Put the vinegar, cloves, cinnamon, honey, lemon and peaches in a saucepan. Bring to a boil then remove from the heat. Let stand for 30 minutes to 1 hour.

Remove the cloves and cinnamon and place the mixture in a blender or food processor. Add the remaining ingredients and blend or process until smooth. Taste for seasoning.

Warm Figs with Honeyed Yogurt

Really good fresh figs are hard to find in the mid south, but they're quite common further on down. I'm mad about them. They're taste is rich and exotic. The cardamom adds an intriguing note, as well.

SERVES 6

12	large fresh figs
4	to 5 tablespoons sugar
½	cup water
3	pods cardamom

HONEYED YOGURT:

12	ounces yogurt
3	ounces honey

Preheat the oven to 325°. Rinse the figs. Stand them upright and touching one another in a baking dish. Pour the water around them and scatter the cardamom around. Bake about 30 minutes.

Stir together the yogurt and honey in a small bowl.

Serve the figs warm, two each in sherbet glasses with the Honeyed Yogurt.

Benne Cookies

I always like to have cookies to pass after a meal. These are a Low Country classic.

MAKES ABOUT 48 COOKIES

¾	cup sesame seeds
½	cup butter, at room temperature
1	cup firmly packed brown sugar
1	egg
1	teaspoon vanilla extract
1	cup all-purpose flour
¼	teaspoon baking powder
	Pinch salt

Preheat the oven to 350°. Place the sesame seeds on a baking sheet and toast in the oven for about 5 minutes. Be careful not to burn. Reduce the heat to 325°.

Beat together the butter and brown sugar until light and fluffy. Beat in the egg and then stir in the vanilla. Sift together the flour, baking powder, and salt, and mix into the liquid mixture. Stir in the sesame seeds and mix well.

Place small spoonfuls of the batter 2 inches apart on greased baking sheets. Bake about 5 to 7 minutes or until slightly spread out and browned. Let the cookies cool and set on the baking sheets. Store in an airtight container for 3 to 4 days.

3.

Dinner Under A Thousand Stars

*T*he skies seem to open up in September. Incredibly clear and bright blue days, and a blanket of stars at night. I'll never forget seeing my first shooting star on a September night when I was seventeen. I was at my senior class retreat, lying on my back in the grass, sharing secrets and grand ambitions with two of my closest friends, when a flash flew across the sky and straight off the page. "Did you see that?" We felt like we had witnessed a miracle. We stayed there forever and counted seven shooting stars that night. To this day, on a clear September night, you can barely keep me inside. If I were still seventeen, I'd spend every evening lying on my back in the grass, gazing upwards to catch the shooting stars.

We eat on the patio as often as possible during the weeks between the heat and the cold, making good use of the grill. I try to keep things simple, so I can spend as much time as possible out of the kitchen. A meal outside always makes you want to eat a little more, linger a little longer. Put your feet up and lean your head back. Maybe clasp a nearby hand and share a grand ambition.

The Menu

Spiced Pecans

———

Marinated Grilled Quail or Dove

———

Refried October Beans

———

Wilted Mustard Greens

———

Grilled Bread with Herbed Goat Cheese

———

Potato Cup Cakes with Cream Cheese Icing

Spiced Pecans

Pecans are probably the *southern nut. I love the spiced ones from Mingo River in South Carolina, but they're easy to do yourself, and you can vary the taste. These are pretty basic, but very good. I like to keep them on hand for my evening nibble.*

MAKES 1 QUART

1	quart pecan halves
½	cup butter
¼	teaspoon cayenne pepper
	Salt to taste

Preheat the oven to 250°. Spread the pecans on a baking sheet and dot with the butter. Bake for about 1 hour, stirring occasionally, until nicely browned. Remove from the oven and sprinkle with the cayenne and salt. Stir and let cool. Store in a tin.

Marinated Grilled Quail or Dove

Dove season opens in September, and the woods are full of them. There's a short quail season, too, but you can buy farm-raised quail year round. I particularly like dove on the grill. They're frequently wrapped in bacon, but its not necessary with this tasty marinade.

SERVES 6

1	cup dry red wine
	juice of 1 lemon
½	cup olive oil
1	bay leaf
1	teaspoon mustard powder
2	cloves garlic, crushed
1	teaspoon salt
½	teaspoon cracked black pepper
12	partially deboned quail

Mix together everything but the quail in a large bowl or Pyrex dish. Add the quail, turning to coat all sides well. Cover and marinate in the refrigerator for at least 1 hour or up to 8 hours.

Prepare the grill. Remove the quail from the refrigerator. Grill for about 4 minutes per side until nicely browned or to your own liking.

Refried October Beans

October beans start in August and run through part of October. I cook them a hundred ways. This is a variation of Mexican beans, mashed in a skillet. You can do them ahead of time and reheat them in the microwave, if you like. These are rich and creamy.

SERVES 6

2	pounds fresh October beans
1	teaspoon salt, or to taste
1	fresh or dry cayenne pepper
3	to 4 tablespoons olive oil
½	yellow onion, diced
3	cloves garlic, chopped

Bring a large pot of water to boil with salt. Add the beans, bay leaf and pepper. Cook about 20 minutes or until the beans tender. Remove from the heat, but do not drain.

Heat the olive oil in a large heavy skillet. Add the onions and brown for 10 minutes. Add the garlic and cook 1 minute more. Use a slotted spoon to spoon out about a third of the beans and place them in the skillet. Mash down with the back of a wooden spoon. Repeat twice, using all of the beans. Stir in about a cup of the cooking water. Cook over low heat about 5 minutes. Adjust the seasonings and serve.

Wilted Mustard Greens

Mustard greens have a delicate leaf and can be cooked quite briefly. Their peppery taste is great with lemon.

SERVES 6

1	bunch mustard greens
3	slices bacon
½	small red onion, chopped
	Juice of two lemons
	Salt and pepper to taste

Trim and clean the greens well. Roughly chop. Cook the bacon in a large skillet until crispy. Remove the bacon and drain on paper towels. Add the red onion to the skillet and cook briefly, until it starts to brown. Add the greens to the skillet and stir. Cook until they are wilted and just tender. Squeeze in the lemon juice, and season with salt and pepper. Serve hot with the bacon crumbled on top.

Grilled Bread with Herbed Goat Cheese

Bread picks up a wonderful smoky aroma and taste when you briefly grill the slices. My daughter Moriah especially likes it this way. Her Daddy is the Executive Chef at Provence, the best bakery in Nashville, which makes beautiful, artisan style loaves. It takes a bread of some substance to grill, sliced a little thick. The goat cheese will spread and taste better if you bring it to room temperature.

SERVES 6

8	ounces soft goat cheese
1	teaspoon fresh thyme leaves
2	teaspoons chopped fresh parsley
6	slices good sourdough bread
	Olive oil

Mix the goat cheese with the herbs and set aside.

Brush the bread with a little olive oil and toast lightly on both sides. Spread the toast with the goat cheese and serve at once.

Potato Cup Cakes with Cream Cheese Icing

This is a very old-fashioned recipe for a super moist cake. Most people think of cup cakes as just for kids, but I like them any time for anyone. What could be more festive than having your own specially decorated cake, just for you? Sometimes I really personalize them with names or monograms written in icing on each.

MAKES ABOUT 10 CUPCAKES

1	baking potato
2	cups sugar
1	cup butter, softened
4	eggs
1	teaspoon vanilla extract
2	cups all-purpose flour
2	teaspoons baking powder
½	cup Dutch process cocoa
1	teaspoon cinnamon
¼	teaspoon cloves
1	cup walnut pieces
½	cup milk
	Cream Cheese Icing (recipe follows)

Preheat the oven to 350°. Line a muffin tin with paper cups. Bake the potato until quite soft. Peel and mash very well by hand or put through a ricer. Set aside. Cream together the sugar and the butter. Beat the eggs and mix in. Add the potatoes and vanilla and mix well. Sift together the dry ingredients. Add alternately with the milk, beginning and ending with the flour mixture. Add the nuts and mix.

Pour the batter into the cups and bake about 20 minutes. Allow to cool before frosting.

Cream Cheese Icing

MAKES 2½ CUPS

8	ounces cream cheese, softened
1	cup butter, softened
1½	teaspoon vanilla extract
4	cups sifted confectioner's sugar

Blend the cream cheese and butter together until very smooth. Add the vanilla and confectioner's sugar, beating until smooth. Frost the cooled cup cakes with the frosting.

4.

Slow Down Supper

Just a few weeks into the school season, and already life can seem pretty crazy. Classes and clubs fit somewhere in the schedule, and for parents, work's almost always busier. It seems we're even now gearing up for the holiday season looming ahead. As a still relatively new mother, I've already discovered that on the evenings when I take the time to prepare even a simple homemade supper and bring us together at the table, our whole dynamic as a family and individuals is refreshed. We look at one another and smile. We talk and share our day's experience.

This meal is an easy one, made special by a delicious selection of seafood. Always buy the freshest. If you're going to splurge anywhere, I would do it in seafood. Where we live, it's expensive because of shipping. My friend Keith grew up in New Orleans and now runs a refrigerated truck between New Orleans and Nashville twice a week. Then there's Kerim, an emigre from Turkey. He's fanatical about quality. He picks up whole tuna and swordfish at the airport and cuts them up at the store where I work. The best sushi bars in town all buy from Kerim. I figure that's a good sign. Wherever you may buy, its a good idea to make the fish monger your friend, and always take a good whiff. Really good fish doesn't smell fishy, but clean and bright.

The Menu

Creole Fisherman's Stew

———

Your Basic Popcorn Rice

———

The Simplest Salad

———

Savory Corn Sticks

———

Gingerbread with Lemon Glaze

Creole Fisherman's Stew

This is a quick stew that's good over rice or pasta, or served alone, more as a soup. You can certainly vary the seafood, or substitute chicken or sausages.

SERVES 6

3	tablespoons olive oil
1	yellow onion, diced
3	cloves garlic, chopped
½	red bell pepper, diced
½	green bell pepper, diced
2	stalks celery, sliced
1	32-ounce can tomatoes
½	cup dry white wine
½	cup chicken or fish stock
2	teaspoons salt
½	teaspoon black pepper
¼	teaspoon white pepper
½	teaspoon red pepper
1	teaspoon fresh thyme leaves (½ teaspoon dried)
1	teaspoon fresh oregano (½ teaspoon dried)
1	bay leaf
1	pound peeled and deveined shrimp
1	pound white fleshed fish, such as snapper or grouper, cut into 2-inch pieces
1	pound scallops

Heat the olive oil in a large, heavy saucepan. Add the onion and cook on high heat about 4 minutes. Add the peppers and celery and cook another 4 minutes. Add the garlic and continue to cook another minute or so. Add the tomatoes with their juice. Break up the tomatoes. Add the wine, stock, salt and peppers, and herbs. Bring the mixture to a boil, and then reduce the heat to medium. Cook another 10 minutes. Add the seafood. Stir lightly to submerge into the sauce. Cook for 5 to 10 minutes or until the seafood is done. Serve over baked rice.

Your Basic Popcorn Rice

Popcorn rice is a variety grown in Louisiana, so named because your house will smell just like popcorn when it's cooking. My mother likes to boil, rinse, then slowly steam popcorn rice to separate every kernel. I rarely have the patience. This is very good, and a lot more simple.

Serves 6 to 8

2	tablespoons butter or olive oil
2	cups popcorn rice
4	cups water
1	teaspoon salt, or to taste

Melt the butter in a heavy saucepan. Add the rice and stir to coat. Add the water and salt and stir. Bring to boil, and stir. Cover and reduce the heat to very low. Cook for 15 to 18 minutes. Fluff with a fork and serve.

The Simplest Salad

With tender leaves like Boston and Bibb, a gentle approach is the best. This is one of my favorite salads. Like Audrey Hepburn or Jackie O., simple, chic, and tasty.

SERVES 6

2	*heads bibb or butter lettuce*
2	*to 3 tablespoons very good olive oil*
	Juice of 1 lemon
	Sprinkle of salt
	Sprinkle of freshly cracked black pepper

Wash and dry the lettuce, treating it gently and keeping it intact. Cut each head into sixths. Place two sections on each plate. Drizzle with a teaspoon or two of oil, squeeze the lemon over it, and garnish with salt and pepper. Serve at once.

Savory Corn Sticks

The onions in these give an added dimension of flavor.

SERVES 6 TO 8

1	tablespoon shortening or bacon fat
½	yellow onion, diced
1¾	cups white cornmeal
1	teaspoon baking powder
1	teaspoon baking soda
¾	teaspoons salt
2	eggs
2	cups buttermilk

Preheat the oven to 400°. Use a paper towel to generously wipe oil over a corn stick pan. Melt the shortening or fat in a skillet. Add the onion and cook about 5 minutes until translucent. Stir together the cornmeal, baking powder, soda, and salt. Beat the eggs with the milk and stir into the dry ingredients. Add the fat and the onions, and stir well. Use a ladle to spoon the batter into the prepared corn stick pan, about two-thirds up the side. Bake for 10 to 15 minutes until golden brown.

5.

Harvest Moon Grill

*I*s anything in the world more festive than a hayride? Perhaps, but not in Autumn. So many good things combined. The smells of horses and the earth. The evening air against your cheek. The tickle, tickle of fresh hay as it pushes through your sweater and into your shoes. Silly songs, sung off-key. And, my favorite part, the promise of a wonderful campfire meal at the end of your sojourn. Then maybe some ghost stories.

My friend Kay's grandmother had a farm when we were in high school, in what we all thought were the outskirts of town. Hayrides were a much anticipated harvest moon event. There are a dozen huge houses standing today where that farm was fifteen years ago. I do hope that the spirit of our high school frolics remains on those acres in some fashion for some time to come.

This is a fantastic fall outside grill, hayride or not. Warm and savory flavors to accentuate the chill in the air.

The Menu

Rubbed and Grilled Pork Tenderloin

———

Skillet Fried Cabbage

———

Sweet Potato Mash

———

Fried Corn Bread with Parm

———

Applesauce Cake with Orange Blossom Cream

Rubbed and Grilled Pork Tenderloin

A rub is a wonderful way to add flavor to any meat. Toasting and grinding seeds will get you more intense flavor. Don't be intimidated. It's a very simple process that takes just a couple of minutes. I have one coffee grinder for coffee and one for spices. It's the perfect size and takes up little room. If your really in a hurry, however, you can always use powdered spices. But once you toast them yourself, you'll never go back!

SERVES 6 TO 8

4	pork tenderloins (they usually come packed 2 per container)
1	tablespoon cumin seeds (or 2 teaspoons powder)
1	tablespoon mustard seeds (or 2 teaspoons dry)
½	cup cracked black peppercorns
2	tablespoons crushed red pepper
2	tablespoons brown mustard
¼	cup salt

Rinse the tenderloins and pat dry. Use a boning or paring knife to remove the silver skin—the shiny membrane covering a portion of the meat. Set the meat aside and prepare the rub.

If you are using the cumin and mustard seeds, place them in a small skillet on top of the stove on high heat. Toast them until they begin to pop. Pour them directly into a spice mill (or clean electric coffee grinder) and grind to a powder. Combine in a bowl with the remaining ingredients and stir to mix. Rub the spice mix onto the pork evenly, pressing the mixture into the skin. Refrigerate for at least 1 hour and up to 24 (the longer the spice mix is on the pork, the more flavor the pork will absorb throughout the meat). Refrigerate until ready to grill.

Prepare the grill. Cook the tenderloins for about 6 minutes per side for medium, 8 to 10 for more well cooked pork. Let stand for 5 minutes before slicing. Serve over the Skillet Fried Cabbage.

Skillet Fried Cabbage

I am fond of cabbage, and it's oh, so good for you. This preparation is fast and delicious. In this meal it serves as a sort of relish for the pork.

SERVES 6 TO 8

2	to 3 tablespoons olive oil
1	red onion, thinly sliced
½	head green cabbage, sliced thinly
2	cloves garlic, chopped
	Juice and zest of 1 lemon
1	to 2 tablespoons cider vinegar
½	teaspoons salt, or to taste
¼	teaspoons red pepper flakes, or to taste

Heat the oil in a skillet. Add the onion and cook a couple of minutes. Toss in the cabbage and garlic and cook on high for about 5 minutes. Add the lemon juice, vinegar, salt and pepper and cook a minute or two more. Stir in the lemon zest and serve warm.

Sweet Potato Mash

Yum, yum! Rich and creamy, but somewhat tart thanks to the Granny Smiths.

SERVES 6 TO 8

4	sweet potatoes, peeled and cut large dice
2	tart apples, such as Granny Smith, cored and diced large
½	yellow onion, diced large
½	cup maple syrup
	Salt and white pepper to taste
	Cayenne to taste (optional)
4	tablespoons butter, cut in small pieces

Preheat the oven to 350°. Combine all the ingredients except the butter in a greased baking dish, and dot the top with the butter. Cover the pan with foil and bake about 25 minutes.

Stir the ingredients, cover again, and continue baking until everything is very soft, about 20 or so more minutes.

Turn out into a mixing bowl and roughly mash (I like to leave some lumps). Taste and adjust the seasoning. Serve hot.

Fried Cornbread with Parm

This is simply the hot water corn bread from my first book with the addition of Parmesan cheese, cutting back on the salt. The cheese gives the bread a richer taste. I like it both ways.

MAKES ABOUT 12 SMALL PIECES OF CORN BREAD

2	cups good cornmeal
½	cup Parmesan cheese
¼	teaspoon salt
	Vegetable oil for frying

Heat about ½-inch of oil in a large skillet. Stir the cornmeal, salt, and Parmesan cheese together in a bowl. Pour the hot water over the meal and stir together to a thick mash. Drop by spoonfuls into the oil and fry until golden brown all over. Drain on a clean brown paper bag and sprinkle with a touch more salt. Serve warm or room temperature.

Applesauce Cake

Such a homey dessert, and delicious, too. If you can't find orange blossom water (most specialty stores have it), simple, lightly sweetened whipped cream, sour cream, or even ice cream will do nicely.

SERVES 14

3	cups all-purpose flour
1½	teaspoons baking soda
2	teaspoons ground cinnamon
½	teaspoon allspice
½	teaspoon nutmeg
1	teaspoon salt
1	cup butter
1¾	cups firmly packed light brown sugar
2	eggs
2	cups very good, unsweetened applesauce (preferably homemade)
1	cup black or English walnut pieces
1	cup raisins
1	teaspoon vanilla extract
	Confectioners' sugar for dusting

Grease and flour a 9-inch bundt pan. Preheat the oven to 325°.

Sift together the dry ingredients and set aside. Cream the butter and sugar together. Beat in the eggs. Fold in half of the dry ingredients, then the applesauce, then the other half of the dry ingredients. Stir in the walnut, raisins and vanilla. Pour the batter into the prepared pan and bake in the middle of the oven for about 1 hour and 30 minutes or until a toothpick inserted in the cake comes out clean.

Allow the cake to cool in the pan. Tap the sides of the pan against the counter top to loosen. Place a serving platter over and invert. If any of the cake sticks to the pan, just lift it out and stick it in place. Dust well with confectioners' sugar and serve with Orange Blossom Cream (recipe follows).

Orange Blossom Cream

WHIPS TO ABOUT 1 PINT

1	cup heavy whipping cream
4	tablespoons confectioners' sugar
½	teaspoon orange blossom water

If whipping by hand, be sure the cream is very cold. You may place the bowl and whip in the refrigerator for 30 minutes prior. Whip the cream to soft peaks. Add the sugar and orange blossom water and whip until almost stiff.

OCTOBER

October is when the ghouls descend! Flirtatious breezes swirl the falling leaves and lift the hems of little girls' skirts. It's sweater weather for raking leaves, horseback riding, and holding hands. Cheeks turn as rosy as the apples we fry, toss in salads, and munch upon. Appetites return with the chill in the air, calling for hardier picnics and breakfast fare. Just a few more days are left to bundle up on the porch and watch the geese fly across the lake. Pumpkins, greens, and hard-fleshed squash take over the farmers' market, along with big pots of jewel-toned chrysanthemums. Is that the Bell Witch whispering through the leaves, or maybe just little ghouls scheming at foul play?

6.

Supper with My Sisters

*M*y sisters are my closest friends. Now more than ever, with our children fairly ador-

ing one another. Sallie's Richard is the oldest and responsible member of the group.

He's amazing with my daughter Moriah and Mary's son Keith, four months apart, who

stomp loudly in place and scream at the top of their lungs when they see one another.

This means that they're happy. They both worship Richard. He does his best to keep

them from waking Phelps, Mary's newborn. My sisters and I are nowhere more com-

fortable than in one of our three homes. Cooking is not something we want to be

messing with when there are children to be chased, so we like to prepare do-ahead-

dishes. That, and have a spot of wine to soothe the nerves.

The Menu

Chicken and Potato Pot

———

Toasted Brussels Sprouts

———

Applesauce with Cranberries

———

Honey Custards

———

Grape Conserve

Chicken and Potato Pot

Actually, I was taught to make this in the Virgin Islands by a lady named Sylvie from Martinique. She referred to it as "bonne femme," or "good wife." This phrase applies to simple and hearty cooking, just like home-cooked southern food. You could assemble this in the morning and refrigerate most of the day. About an hour before supper proceed with baking. Your house will smell divine.

SERVES 4 TO 6

1	tablespoon olive oil
1	pound Yukon Gold potatoes, cleaned and sliced about ¼-inch
1	large onion, diced
3	cloves garlic, chopped
	Juice of 2 lemons
1	tablespoon chopped fresh parsley
2	teaspoons fresh thyme leaves
¼	teaspoon salt
¼	teaspoon black pepper
1	3- to 4-pound chicken, cut up; or 6 bone in, skin on breasts or leg quarters
	Salt and black and red pepper to taste

Pour the oil in the bottom of a 2-quart ovenproof baking dish. Scatter the potatoes, onions, and garlic over the oil. Squeeze over the lemon juice, sprinkle the herbs, salt, and pepper. Give it all a good stir.

Season the chicken with additional salt and pepper and settle the pieces over the potatoes. Cover with foil and bake about 30 minutes. Remove the foil and bake another 30 minutes. Serve warm.

Toasted Brussels Sprouts

Mary won't like this. She doesn't do Brussels sprouts, as she says. We'll make her a simple green salad. Sally and I adore Brussels sprouts, and they're perfect with the rest of the meal. Moriah likes them, too.

SERVES 6

2	pounds Brussels sprouts, cleaned, trimmed and cut in half
1	teaspoon salt
3	tablespoons butter
	Juice of 1 lemon
4	tablespoons fresh bread crumbs
4	tablespoons Parmesan or other grating cheese
1	tablespoon chopped fresh parsley
	Salt and pepper to taste

Bring a large pot of water to boil with the teaspoon salt. Add the Brussels sprouts and cook about 10 minutes until tender. Drain and place in a baking dish. Toss with the butter to melt. Preheat the oven to broil. Mix the bread crumbs with the Parmesan, parsley, salt, and pepper. Sprinkle over the Brussels sprouts and broil about 5 minutes until browned. Serve warm.

Applesauce with Cranberries

The cranberries make this a gorgeous color and add a nice tart flavor. Make lots and keep it on hand to perk up every supper.

SERVES 6 TO 8

4	pounds cooking apples, peeled and cut large dice
1	pound cranberries, rinsed
¾	cup apple juice
1	tablespoon grated fresh ginger

Place all in a heavy saucepan and bring to a boil. Reduce the heat and cook on medium for about 30 minutes, stirring occasionally. Let cool. May be refrigerated for at least a week.

Honey Custards

Cold dessert custards are rarely seen these days, except for the Spanish custard, flan. Well, custards know no geographical borders and were once quite common throughout the states. I like them for their simple taste and soothing texture. This one with honey has an added richness.

SERVES 6

2	cups heavy cream
4	egg yolks
¼	cup honey
1	teaspoon vanilla extract

Preheat the oven to 325°. Prepare six ½-cup custard or soufflé cups by buttering generously.

Bring the cream to a boil, being careful not to scorch it. Remove it from the heat and let it sit for 5 minutes. Beat together the eggs and the honey. Pour a bit of the cream into the egg mixture and stir. Now pour the egg mixture into the cream, stirring. Add the vanilla and stir. Pour the custard into the cups. Place the cups in a shallow baking pan and fill the pan half way up the sides of the cups with boiling water. Bake the custards for 40 minutes. Remove from the water and let cool. Refrigerate until ready to use.

Serve in the cups or unmold onto dessert plates. Spoon over or pass the Grape Conserve (recipe follows).

Grape Conserve

Wonderful for dessert or with toast for breakfast.

MAKES ABOUT 3 CUPS

2	navel oranges
½	cup apple cider
1½	pounds seedless grapes
2	cups sugar
½	cup lemon juice
1	teaspoon cinnamon

Cut the oranges in thin circles and quarter these. Place in a heavy pan with the cider and cook about 15 minutes until the peel is soft. Add the remaining ingredients and cook about 30 or 40 minutes until thickened. Let cool and refrigerate.

This will keep covered in the refrigerator for two weeks.

7.

Point to Point Picnic

*M*iddle Tennessee is horse country. Belle Meade Plantation bred the finest race horses over a century ago, and many residents of what is now the Belle Meade neighborhood are enthusiasts to this day. Each spring and fall the local hunt clubs sponsor a not-too formal day of point to point racing in the most pastoral of settings, outside of Nashville in Hillsboro.

The most popular event is perhaps the terrier race, with the feisty Jack Russell inevitably taking the lead. I must say, though, that ever since a Jack Russell fairly bit off the end of my passive and amicable 120-pound bloodhound's nose on one fine point to point morn, I haven't felt quite the same about the sporty little beast, but they do make for a spirited chase.

My purpose, as usual, is to feed the hungry. This is not a snooty menu, as some tail gates can be. Just good honest food that packs and unpacks quite well. Tastes good, too.

The Menu

Roasted Chicken Sandwich, Spicy and Good

———

Hot Green Mustard Mayonnaise

———

Broccoli and Blue Cheese Salad

———

Potato and Turnip Salad

———

Ginger Pear Compote

———

Hedgehogs

Roasted Chicken Sandwich, Spicy and Good

Roast the chicken yourself, or pick it up at the store, if you're short of time. I like to use sour-dough bread for the flavor and because it's sturdy enough to withstand travel and time.

SERVES 4 TO 6

1   roasted chicken
    Sourdough bread
    Hot Green Mustard Mayonnaise *(recipe follows)*
    Red onion circles
    Roasted red peppers
    Green leaf lettuce

Cut the breasts from the chicken and slice. Pull away the thighs and pull off nice chunks of meat. Spread the bread with the Hot Green Mustard Mayonnaise. Pile high with plenty of chicken and garnish with the other ingredients. Cut in half. These will keep for several hours, wrapped in plastic.

Hot Green Mustard Mayonnaise

The mustard here is fresh mustard greens. Vibrant color and taste.

MAKES ABOUT 1½ PINTS

2	*tablespoons lemon juice*
1	*teaspoon salt*
1	*clove garlic, minced*
1	*small fresh or pickled cayenne pepper, minced*
3	*tablespoons fresh mustard greens, cleaned and coarsely chopped (a good handful of leaves)*
	Pinch black pepper
2	*egg yolks*
1	*pint vegetable oil*

Stir together the lemon juice, salt, garlic, pepper, and chopped mustard greens in a mixing bowl. Place the yolks in the bowl and beat with an electric mixer. Pour in the oil in a thin steady stream. The oil should "catch" and emulsify. The more oil you add, the thicker the mayonnaise. Pour in all the oil, then taste and adjust the seasoning.

This will keep in the refrigerator for at least a week.

Broccoli and Blue Cheese Salad

Assertive flavors seem correct on a brisk day.

SERVES 6

1	bunch broccoli
1	tablespoon salt
½	red onion, diced
2	cloves garlic, minced
½	cup sour cream
¼	cup crumbled blue cheese
	Juice of 2 lemons
¼	teaspoon cayenne pepper
¼	cup toasted almond slices

Bring a large pot of water with the salt to a boil. Add the broccoli and cook uncovered for 3 minutes. Drain and cool the broccoli completely under cold water.

Place the broccoli in a mixing bowl along with the onion. In a separate bowl stir together the garlic, sour cream, blue cheese, lemon juice, pepper, and salt to taste. Mix with the broccoli and onion. Stir in the almonds. Serve at room temperature.

Potato and Turnip Salad

Turnips give this salad a little twang, an added dimension.

SERVES 6

1	pound Yukon Gold potatoes
1	pound turnips
3	tablespoons olive oil
1	tablespoon dijon mustard
1	tablespoon white wine vinegar
1	tablespoon chopped fresh parsley
	Salt and pepper to taste

Scrub the potatoes and cook in boiling salted water about 10 to 15 minutes until tender and cooked through.

Peel the turnips and cook in a separate pot of boiling salted water until tender and cooked through, more like 7 to 10 minutes. Drain both and place together in a mixing bowl (do not rinse or cool). Mix together the olive oil, mustard, vinegar, and parsley, and pour over the potatoes and turnips. Stir lightly to mix. Serve either warm or cool (not cold).

Ginger Pear Compote

I use this dish as a room temperature or cool side dish, but it is also wonderful served warm with ice cream for dessert.

SERVES 6

	Juice and peel of 2 lemons
1½	quarts water
¾	cup sugar
1	2-inch piece fresh ginger, peeled and sliced fairly thin
2	pounds just ripe or slightly under ripe pears

Take the peel from the lemon with a carrot peeler. Start the water heating with the juice from the lemon, the peel, sugar, and ginger. Stir to dissolve the sugar, and bring the liquid to a boil. Lower the heat to simmer. Peel, core, and cut the pears into large dice, about 1 inch, dropping the pear pieces into the the syrup as you work. Once all the pears are in the syrup, let simmer for 30 minutes. Remove the pears from the syrup and place in a bowl. Continue to simmer the syrup until reduced by half. Remove from the heat and pour over the pears in the bowl. Let cool, cover, and refrigerate.

Hedgehogs

The silly name refers to their appearance. They taste great and travel well.

MAKES 1 DOZEN

2	cups walnuts
2	eggs
1	cup firmly packed dark brown sugar
1	cup pitted dates, chopped
1	cup shredded coconut

Preheat the oven to 350°. Grease a cookie sheet. Place the nuts in a food processor and process fine. Beat the eggs with the sugar and mix in the dates. Stir in the nuts and ¾ cup of the coconut. Shape into ovals about 1-inch long and ½-inch wide. Roll each cookie in the remaining coconut. Place on the greased cookie sheet and bake for 15 minutes.

Roasted Chicken Sandwich, Spicy and Good

Broiled Oysters with Beet Vinaigrette

Mushroom and Sausage Pie with Cornmeal Crust

Sweet Milk Drop Biscuits

8.

Oysters for Sallie

Sallie's husband Sammy gets a little nervous when Sallie and I get together to cook. The reason is two fold. Sammy's not really big on unusual vegetables, and Sallie and I are most intent on slipping in an evil beet or mushroom when we don't think he'll notice. He usually does. And then there's the matter of clean up, of which Sammy is in charge. From our childhood on, Sallie and I have approached cooking with the wild abandon of Isadora Duncan on stage. Unfortunately, our stage gets a little messier than Ms. Duncan's did. Several years in the food biz and a couple of children under our belts have tidied us up a bit, but I still see the fear in Sammy's eyes when we say we're trying something new.

This year, Mama and Daddy volunteered their house for Sallie's birthday event, and I volunteered my services. I tried to think of all of Sallie's favorite things, but there are just too many. It would have been like dining with Caligula, so I narrowed down the list and celebrated the bounty of the season along with her special day. Happy birthday, Sal!

The Menu

Chicken and Apple Sausages with Ginger, Garlic, and Mint

———

Broiled Oysters with Beet Vinaigrette

———

Baked Hominy with Mushrooms

———

Spinach Salad with Red Grapes and Pumpkin Seeds and Goat Cheese Vinaigrette

———

Maple Brown Sugar Sour Cream Pound Cake

———

Dried Apricot and Vanilla Bean Ice Cream

Chicken and Apple Sausage with Ginger, Garlic, and Mint

I love this sausage, and its really easy to make. A couple of things to think about with raw ground meats (particularly chicken): always keep the meat quite cold. Don't allow it to sit out for too long. Clean all work surfaces and your hands immaculately. Be sure to cook the patties thoroughly.

When I don't use all of the sausage at once, I make up the remaining patties, wrap them individually in plastic and freeze them. I'm always delighted to find them on Sunday morning (or Monday night, for that matter). I just thaw in the microwave before frying.

MAKES ABOUT 2 POUNDS

2¼	pounds bone-in, skin-on chicken thighs
½	ounce dried apples, diced
2	tablespoons minced fresh ginger (about a 2-inch piece)
1	tablespoon minced fresh garlic (about 3 cloves)
2½	teaspoons salt
1	teaspoon red pepper flakes
½	teaspoon black pepper
3	tablespoons chopped fresh mint leaves
2	teaspoons corn syrup

De-bone the chicken thighs. Remove the skin from half of them, and cut the meat and skin in about 1-inch cubes. Place in a food processor and pulse until you get the consistency of ground meat. Cover and chill the meat while you prepare the other ingredients. When everything is prepared, place all ingredients together in a mixing bowl and stir well with a rubber spatula or wooden spoon to completely combine. Use your hands to shape into patties. Put just a dash of vegetable oil in a skillet and cook the patties on medium low, turning once and browning both sides. If they brown quickly and are not completely cooked in the center, place the skillet in a hot oven and finish cooking them there. They should cook about 10 minutes. I like to wrap patties individually in plastic wrap and store them in the freezer, where they keep for at least a month.

Broiled Oysters

Ice cold raw oysters are also nice with the Beet Vinaigrette, but in October I like them warmed a bit, plus they pick up a bit of smoky flavor on the grill with the sausages. I have put unopened oysters on the grill before, and the heat popped them open a bit, making it easier to completely remove the top shell. The drawback is that you have to work quickly so they don't overcook, and there's a good chance of burning yourself with hot oyster water seeping out of the shell. I prefer to shell them while they're cold and my guests aren't eying the grill with hunger. Remove the top shell and slip a knife underneath the oyster, completely detaching it from the bottom shell, then place the oysters in the bottom shell directly on the grill, and cover it. You can also broil them in the oven. They should warm through within 5 minutes. If they overcook, they get really tough. Place the warmed oysters on a platter and spoon a little of the Beet Vinaigrette over each.

Beet Vinaigrette

A stunning color and refreshing taste, this vinaigrette is equally nice with a green salad and hard-boiled eggs.

MAKES 2 TO 3 CUPS, ENOUGH FOR ABOUT 3 DOZEN OYSTERS

2	medium beets
1	clove garlic, minced
2	tablespoons roughly chopped flat leaf parsley
2	teaspoons capers
	Zest and juice of 1 lemon
4	tablespoons olive oil
2	teaspoons red wine vinegar
	Salt and freshly cracked black pepper to taste

Trim the ends of the beets and boil in salted water for about 15 or 20 minutes or until just cooked through. Drain and cool. Remove the skin. Place a grater over a mixing bowl, and grate the beets on the medium side of the grater. Add the remaining ingredients and mix well. Refrigerate until 30 minutes prior to use, allowing the vinaigrette to come back to room temperature before using.

Baked Hominy with Mushrooms

This dish has a real depth of flavor without being too rich. Hominy, which is hulled and dried corn, was once the traditional way to enjoy corn year round. You may boil dried hominy, if you like. It's called posole and is available in Latin markets. The canned works just fine, though.

SERVES 8

3	tablespoons olive oil
1	medium yellow onion, diced
1	stick celery, diced
1	carrot, diced
4	cloves garlic, minced
½	pound mushrooms, sliced thin
1	teaspoon minced fresh sage
1	teaspoon fresh thyme leaves
1	32-ounce can hominy, drained
1	cup chicken stock
1	cup heavy cream or milk
½	teaspoon salt (or to taste)
	Black pepper to taste
½	cup dry bread crumbs
2	tablespoons butter, in small pieces

Preheat the oven to 375°. Heat the olive oil in a sauté pan or skillet and add the onion. Cook about 5 minutes until soft. Add the celery and carrot, and cook 5 more minutes. Add the garlic and mushrooms and cook 2 minutes. Remove from the heat and place the vegetables in a casserole. Add the fresh herbs and drained hominy, and stir to combine. Stir together the stock and milk, and stir this into the hominy. Taste and adjust the seasoning. Sprinkle the top with the bread crumbs and dot with the butter. Place in the preheated oven and bake for 30 minutes or until the casserole is set and the top is browned and crispy.

Spinach Salad with Red Grapes and Pumpkin Seeds

A simple fall salad with a great combination of texture and taste.

SERVES 6

1	pound salad or baby spinach
½	cup Goat Cheese Vinaigrette (recipe follows)
	Small bunch red grapes (about 36 grapes)
3	scallions, sliced thinly
½	cup toasted pumpkin seeds

Clean the spinach and dry well. Place the spinach in a salad bowl and toss with the vinaigrette, coating evenly. Slice the grapes in half and add to the salad. Garnish with the remaining ingredients and serve.

Goat Cheese Vinaigrette

Similar in concept to a creamy blue cheese dressing, but with the lemony, tart flavor of goat cheese.

MAKES 2 CUPS

4	ounces soft goat cheese
4	tablespoons buttermilk
2	cloves garlic minced
3	tablespoons white wine vinegar
¼	teaspoon salt
	Liberal freshly cracked black pepper
1	tablespoon chopped fresh basil
½	cup olive oil

Place the goat cheese in a small mixing bowl and add the buttermilk. Stir to blend. Add the garlic, vinegar, salt, pepper, and basil, and stir well. Whisk in the olive oil. Refrigerate until 30 minutes prior to serving. Stir with a fork to re-emulsify if necessary. Will keep tightly covered in a refrigerator for 1 week.

Maple Brown Sugar Sour Cream Pound Cake

For Sallie's birthday, I filled the center of this bundt cake with a juice glass holding chrysanthemums, and stuck tapered birthday candles around the cake. Very pretty and simple to do.
This cake is velvety dense and not too sweet. The flavors marry perfectly with the dried fruit in the ice cream. It's also a treat toasted for breakfast or tea. Another bonus: it freezes great.

MAKES 1 LARGE BUNDT CAKE OR TWO 9-INCH LOAVES.

2½ cups sifted all-purpose flour
½ teaspoon baking soda
1 cup unsalted butter, softened
2½ cups firmly packed light brown sugar
6 large eggs, separated, at room temperature
1⅓ cups sour cream
2 teaspoons maple flavoring

Preheat the oven to 325°. Butter and flour a large bundt pan. Sift together the flour and baking soda and set aside. Cream the butter and sugar about 3 minutes. Add the egg yolks one at a time, beating well after each. Add half the flour and beat to incorporate, then add half the sour cream and beat. Repeat with the remaining halves. Stir in the maple flavoring. Beat the egg whites until very stiff. Fold one-third into the batter to lighten it. Then gently fold in the remainder. Pour into the prepared pan.
Bake on the center rack of the oven for 1 hour and 10 to 1 hour and 20 minutes until golden brown on top and a cake tester inserted in the center comes out clean. Let the cake cool in the pan.

Dried Apricot and Vanilla Bean Ice Cream

Whole vanilla beans are a little dear, but you can't mistake the added flavor. You'll notice the characteristic tiny black dots from the bean. Very pretty, I think, and a sign that you care enough about your guests to use the real thing.

MAKES A LITTLE OVER 1 QUART

2	cups whole milk
1	vanilla bean, split
6	ounces dried apricots, diced
4	large egg yolks
1	cup superfine sugar
2	cups heavy cream, kept chilled

Pour the milk into a saucepan and add the split vanilla bean. Heat the milk to simmering and remove from the heat. Heat water in the bottom of a double boiler to simmering. Off the heat, place the egg yolks and sugar in the top of the double boiler and whisk together until pale yellow. Slowly pour in the milk, whisking. Place the top of the double over the simmering (not boiling) water and cook, stirring constantly, for 8 to 10 minutes until the custard thickens enough to coat the back of a spoon. Remove from the heat and stir in the apricots. Stir in the chilled cream and refrigerate for at least 30 minutes or overnight.

Pour into an ice cream maker and freeze according to the manufacturer's instructions.

9.

Book Club Pie

I belong to an errant book club. We began with such high hopes and good intentions. Simple, really. Once a month. Read the book or keep your mouth shut. No shouting, please.

Well, we kept up with the once-a-month for quite a while. But some of us (who shall remain unnamed) tended to speak of things of which we knew not. And with a tone of authority, mind you. And some of us, gentle reader, had a tendency to shout. We began to argue about what to read. Were we a literary group, or not? We tended to read southern literature, and then we tended to fight and refight The War. And then there was the night we got into subsidized tobacco farming and you don't want to know what all else.

The constant beneficent quality inherent in our group was, not surprisingly, the quality of the food. We haven't met in oh, so long, but we all are still filled with good intention and genuine affection for one another, shout though we may. This October, I swear we'll meet at my house, and dive in, once again, dive into Book Club Pie.

The Menu

Cheese and Pears

———

Mushroom and Sausage Pie with Cornmeal Crust

———

Warm Beets

———

Cold Collards

———

Pumpkin Ice Cream with Warm Caramel Sauce

Cheese and Pears

Sometimes the simplest things are the best.

4	pears
1	8-ounce wedge blue cheese

Pears begin to pour into the market as fall wears on. There are Bosc, Bartlett, Comice, and D'Anjou, to name but a few. Choose whatever is at its peak of ripeness. Many cheeses are wonderful with pears. I prefer blues. Maytag Blue from Idaho is a particular American favorite. Bring the cheese to room temperature before serving. I like to serve it on a simple plate or tray with a knife so people can help themselves. Surround the cheese with thin slices of pear (cut the pear just before serving) and perhaps some slices of crusty bread. Divine!

Mushroom and Sausage Pie with Cornmeal Crust

Prepare this early in the morning or the day before, but don't bake. When your guests arrive, just pop it in the oven.

SERVES 6 TO 8

FOR THE FILLING:

1 pound mushrooms
1 pound sausage
1 yellow onion, diced
3 cloves garlic, chopped
2 stalks celery, diced
1 carrot , diced
2 tablespoons flour
¼ cup dry white wine
1½ cups chicken stock
1 tablespoon fresh thyme leaves
1 teaspoon fresh sage, minced
    Salt and pepper to taste

FOR THE CRUST:

1¾ cups all-purpose flour
¾ cup yellow cornmeal
1 teaspoon salt
½ pound cold unsalted butter
¼ cup shortening
⅓ to ¼ cup ice water

Clean the mushrooms and cut into quarters. Break up the sausage and place in a large deep skillet or heavy saucepan. Over medium high heat cook the sausage until it renders its fat. Add the onions, garlic, celery, and carrot, and cook about 5 minutes. Add the mushrooms and cook about 5 more minutes until the vegetables are tender. Stir in the flour and cook a couple of minutes, stirring. Add the wine and half of the stock, stirring and working out any lumps. Add the remaining stock and bring the mixture to a boil. Turn the heat to low, add the herbs, salt, and pepper and cook about 10 minutes. Pour into a deep pie dish and set aside until the crust is ready to roll out.

Mix together the flour, meal and salt in a large bowl. Cut the butter into small pieces and quickly cut it into the dry ingredients using either your fingertips or a pastry blender. Add the shortening and continue to work the dough until the texture resembles very coarse meal. Some pea-size pieces of fat may remain. Sprinkle most of the water over the dough and then work it with your hands. The dough should be ragged and fairly difficult to pull together. It's o.k.! Pull the ragged dough together, divide it in half and shape the halves into discs. Wrap these in plastic and refrigerate for at least 30 minutes and up to 24 hours before using.

To assemble and bake the pie, preheat the oven to 375°. Roll one of the discs out to ⅛-inch thickness. Roll the crust onto the rolling pin to pick it up and place it over the filling. Trim the excess and crimp the edges. Cut a few slashes in the top and bake for 30 or so minutes until the crust is golden brown and the insides are bubbly. Serve hot.

Warm Beets

I don't know why we tend to eat beets cold and pickled. They're delightful warm, with so much flavor, a little butter is all they need. Beautiful on the plate.

SERVES 6

2	*pounds beets, small if available*
	Salt and freshly cracked black pepper to taste
3	*tablespoons butter*

Wash and trim the beets. Cook in boiling, salted water about 10 to 15 minutes until tender. Drain and let cool slightly. When cool enough to handle, remove the skin. Heat the butter in a skillet and add the beets to coat. Sprinkle with salt and pepper and serve.

Cold Collards

Collards are one of the healthiest vegetables around, and cooking them relatively quickly helps them to retain their full nutritive value. I love their gutsy taste.

SERVES 6

1	bunch collard greens
3	tablespoons olive oil
1	red onion, sliced thinly
2	cloves garlic, chopped
1	fresh cayenne, minced
	Juice of 1 lemon
1	tablespoon red wine vinegar

Clean the collards very well, remove the very coarse core, cut the leaves in strips, and set aside. In a deep skillet heat the olive oil. Add the onion and cook on high about 2 or or 3 minutes until its starting to brown. Add the collards and sprinkle with the garlic, cayenne, salt, and pepper. Toss the pan until the greens have wilted. Turn the heat to low and add about a cup of water. Cover the pan and cook about 10 minutes until the greens are tender. Remove the lid and turn the heat back to high. Let any remaining water cook out. Add the lemon juice and vinegar. Toss in a bowl and serve at once or let cool.

Pumpkin Ice Cream

I reserve a pastoral image of us all in our perfect kitchens, steaming our fresh pumpkins. It's fun to do when you have the time, but the canned will do just fine.

MAKES ABOUT 2 QUARTS

1	quart cooked pumpkin
1	cup superfine sugar
1	teaspoon cinnamon
¼	teaspoon nutmeg
1	quart cream

Mix the pumpkin with the sugar and spices. Stir in the cream. Refrigerate for 30 minutes or overnight. Freeze in an ice cream freezer according to the manufacturers' directions.

Warm Caramel Sauce

This sauce is very easy and delicious, too. Equally good on cold poached pears.

MAKES ABOUT 2½ CUPS

1	cup packed light brown sugar
1	cup heavy cream
½	cup unsalted butter, cut into bits

Place all in a heavy saucepan over medium heat. Stir and heat until smooth. Serve warm.

10.

Breakfast at the Lake

*M*y sister Mary and her husband Tom have a romantic old farm house by a beautiful lake about an hour from our homes. We're eight hours from the nearest ocean, but you can't walk too far in Middle Tennessee without wading into into fresh water. Their house is rambling and over a century old. It sits up on a hill surrounded by farms and looks down into the lake. They have room for our entire family, and we jump at any invitation to visit. I think I like it the best in October when we bring out the quilts and watch the graceful flight of ducks through a screen of golden maple leaves.

I love the smells of breakfast cooking in the morning. It's really my favorite meal of the day when I have time to prepare it, and time enough to be lazy and digest the rest of the day. This feast would certainly serve as both breakfast and lunch for most folks.

If we were fishermen of any sort, we'd catch these trout. But, being generally skeptical of both our luck and enterprise, I buy them on the way out of town.

The Menu

Beer Batter Trout

———

Baked Eggs with Cheese

———

Apple and Celery Salad

———

Skillet Potatoes

———

Sweet Milk Drop Biscuits

———

Fig Jam

Beer Batter Trout

This makes a wonderful, crispy crust, that's almost as tasty as the fish itself.

SERVES 6

1	12-ounce can beer (the better the beer, the better the trout!)
2	large eggs, lightly beaten
½	cup buttermilk
2½	cups all-purpose flour
6	trout fillets
1	cup cornmeal
1	tablespoon salt
1	tablespoon black pepper
4	cups vegetable oil

Combine the beer, eggs, buttermilk, and 1½ cups of the flour in a mixing bowl. Put the remaining cup of flour on a plate, and the cornmeal on another plate. Stir the salt and pepper into the batter.

Heat the oil to 350° in a large saucepan over high heat. Fry the trout fillets two at a time for 4 to 6 minutes until cooked through and crispy. Drain on clean paper bags and serve immediately with lemon or malt vinegar.

Baked Eggs with Cheese

This is a very easy way to prepare the eggs while you're frying the trout.

SERVES 6

12 eggs
   Salt and pepper to taste
2 cups shredded sharp Cheddar cheese
1 tablespoon chopped parsley
3 scallions, sliced thinly

Grease the bottom and sides of a 3-quart casserole. Break the eggs directly into the casserole, trying not to break any yolks. Sprinkle salt and pepper over the eggs, scatter the cheese over the eggs, and then the herbs. Bake about 10 to 15 minutes until the eggs are set. Serve at once.

Apple and Celery Salad

Wonderfully tart, crunchy and refreshing. A nice light touch with such a filling meal.

SERVES 6

2	Granny Smith apples, cored and thinly sliced
2	ribs of celery, thinly sliced on the diagonal
6	radishes, thinly sliced
	About 1/4 head red cabbage, shredded
3	scallions, thinly sliced on the diagonal
1	fresh cayenne pepper, thinly sliced (optional)
	Juice of 2 lemons
1/4	cup olive oil
1	bunch mint, stemmed, roughly chopped
	Salt and black pepper, to taste

Place everything in a large bowl and toss gently to combine. Serve at once.

Skillet Potatoes

You can boil the potatoes the night before to give yourself a jump start. I crave a splash of hot sauce on these—it's always on the breakfast table.

SERVES 6

2	pounds potatoes (preferably Yukon gold or red skin)
½	green bell pepper, chopped
½	red onion, chopped
1	pint mushrooms, quartered (optional)
2	cloves garlic, chopped
	Salt and pepper to taste
¼	cup olive oil
1	tablespoon chopped fresh parsley

Scrub the potatoes clean and place in a pot. Cover the potatoes with salted water and bring to a boil. Cook about 10 to 15 minutes until just barely tender.

Drain the potatoes and let cool. Do not rinse. When cool enough to handle, cut the potatoes into fairly large chunks. Heat the oil in a large skillet. Add the onions and cook on medium high heat for about 4 minutes. Add the pepper and garlic and cook another four minutes. Add the mushrooms and let cook a few minutes without stirring, allowing them to brown. Sprinkle with salt and pepper and turn over all of the vegetables in the pan, using a large spatula (it's fine for the vegetables to break up—you're just trying to get some even browning). Season again and brown on all sides. Serve at once.

Sweet Milk Drop Biscuits

I sometimes envision canned biscuits as being the demise of southern culture. Real ones make up in under 10 minutes. You don't hear the phrase "sweet milk" much now. Back when people drank a lot of buttermilk, this was the other (regular) stuff.

MAKES ABOUT 18 BISCUITS

2	cups all-purpose flour
1	teaspoon salt
2	teaspoons baking powder
½	teaspoon baking soda
6	tablespoons chilled butter, cut in small pieces
1½	cups whole milk

Preheat the oven to 425°. Sift the dry ingredients into a bowl. Work the butter in with a pastry blender or your fingertips until the butter works down to the size of small peas. Add the milk and stir just enough to mix. Drop by tablespoons onto an ungreased cookie sheet and bake for about 12 minutes until golden.

Fig Jam

This makes a very rich jam. From an old New Orleans recipe.

MAKES ABOUT 3 PINTS

---

4   *pounds fresh figs*
     Juice and zest from 2 oranges (about 1 cup juice)
     Juice and zest from 2 lemons
3   *cups sugar*

Roughly chop the figs and place in a saucepan along with the orange juice. Bring to a simmer and cook, stirring occasionally for 15 minutes. Add the remaining ingredients and cook about 15 more minutes, until a candy thermometer registers 220°. Process in sterilized jars to keep indefinitely, or keep covered in the refrigerator for up to one month.

II.

Halloween for Grown-ups

Halloween is such a great holiday. I approve of any event that encourages people to act silly. The things we'll do with a mask to hide behind. When I was little, we had a game called "Bats in the Belfry." It was a large, plastic haunted castle with a belfry full of orange plastic bats that were hurled into the air when you dropped a marble through the chimney. I think you were supposed to catch them. My ingenious mother employed the contraption for the benefit of the neighborhood spooks. She placed it (she still does) in the middle of the dining room table with a popcorn ball (home-made, of course) in the belfry, replacing the bats. Each spook must catch his popcorn ball as it flies through the air. Smaller spooks are given a little help.

With all of the treats for little spooks on Halloween, I think that the big spooks (that's us, the grown ups) deserve a nice treat, too. Like a homey soup and sandwich with a fruit crisp for dessert. That's my kind of treat!

The Menu

Pumpkin Soup with Mustard Greens

———

Crispy Cornmeal Croutons (see page 156)

———

Grilled Cheese Sammies

———

Pickled Onions

———

Creamy Coleslaw with Fennel and Turnips

———

Pear and Apple Crisp with Ginger

———

Vanilla Cream

Pumpkin Soup with Mustard Greens

This is different from most pumpkin soups I've had. It's not a purée, but stock based, and it's not as sweet as most. The mustard greens give it a nice kick.

MAKES ABOUT THREE QUARTS, TO SERVE 8 TO 10

1	small cooking pumpkin
1	12-ounce can beer
1	ham hock
1	yellow onion, diced
4	cloves garlic, chopped
1	stick cinnamon
2	dry or fresh cayenne peppers
1	tablespoon salt
1	teaspoon black pepper
1	bunch mustard greens, cleaned and chopped
4	tablespoons honey
	Juice of 2 lemons

Cut the pumpkin in half. Scrape out the strings and seeds (save the seeds to toast). Cut the pumpkin in large 2-inch chunks, then cut off the peel. Rinse the ham hock and place in a soup pot with 1½ quarts of water, the beer, the pumpkin, onion, garlic, cinnamon stick, cayenne, salt and pepper. Bring to a boil, and skim off any scum from the ham hock. Stir, lower the heat to medium, and cook until the pumpkin is tender to the point of falling apart, about 1 hour.

Remove the cinnamon stick and add the mustard greens. Cook about 10 minutes more until the greens are tender. Stir in the honey and lemon juice. Taste and adjust the seasoning. Serve hot.

Grilled Cheese Sammies

Grilled cheese sandwiches are one of my greatest vices, and I have no intention of reforming. I used to order them on rye with onions at all-night diners to complete an evening on the town. These days, I make them at home. I like to add a little something to the cheese and bread mix, whether its peppers, pickles or a spicy relish of some sort.

SERVES 6

12	slices sturdy bread, such as sourdough or rye
12	slices or so good Cheddar cheese
6	teaspoons Hot Green Mustard Mayonnaise (optional, p. 80)
6	tablespoons Pickled Onions (optional)
4	tablespoons or more butter or olive oil

Preheat the oven to warm. Spread one slice of bread with the mayo. Top with the cheese, then the onions. Cover with the other slice of bread. Melt and heat half of the butter or oil in a skillet. Turn the heat down a bit add half of the sandwiches. Cook until golden on one side, then flip and cook on the other side. You may have to add a bit more butter or oil. Press down on the bread with a spatula. Remove from the heat and keep warm in the oven while you cook the remaining sandwiches. Serve hot.

Pear and Apple Crisp with Ginger

This has got a lot going on with ginger and bourbon. I usually make a simple crisp, but some-times I just get bored and start mucking about in the cabinet. This time it worked.

SERVES 6 TO 8

3	ounces crystallized ginger, sliced thin
¼	cup bourbon
3	tart apples, cored, peeled, and chopped
3	just ripe pears, cored, peeled, and chopped
1	cup sifted all-purpose flour
¾	cup sugar
½	teaspoon dried cinnamon
¼	teaspoon salt
½	cup butter, softened and cut into bits

Preheat the oven to 350°. Place the ginger in a bowl and pour the bourbon over. Let sit for 15 minutes.

Grease a 7 x 9-inch baking dish and toss in the pears, apples, and ginger with the bourbon, distributing all of the fruit evenly.

Mix together the remaining ingredients with your fingertips until the consistency of cornmeal. Sprinkle evenly over the fruit.

Bake for about 30 minutes until the top is browned and the juices bubbly. Serve warm with the Vanilla Cream (recipe follows).

Vanilla Cream

Vanilla adds an extra dimension to whipped cream.

MAKES 1 PINT

1   cup heavy cream
4   tablespoons confectioners' sugar
1   drop vanilla extract

Be sure the cream is very cold. If you're beating by hand, you may refrigerate the bowl and whisk for 30 minutes prior. Beat the cream to light peaks. Fold in the sugar and vanilla and beat just a little more. A looser cream is preferable here. Refrigerate until ready to use.

NOVEMBER

November is the setting in. Almost all of the leaves are down, except for a sudden flash of yellow that brightens the grey trees. The hunters sallie forth in their waders and down vests, content to spend a cold, wet day in silent solitude. The hills seem quieter, as most of us slow down and move inside. We focus on the home, fires and jigsaw puzzles, checkers and cards, and baking of bread—any amusement to lessen TV time. Things quiet down at the market. There are turnips and beets and cabbage, still some greens and squash, apples and pears. This is the month to catch our breaths and bring our families together, both immediate and extended. This is the time when I look back over the year and ponder where it has gone and what I have done with it. I count my blessings and give thanks for my wealth: family and friends, hands around the table.

12.

Birthday Brunch for Nana

What doesn't Nana do for us? As she is quick to tell you, she waited way too long to be a grandmother, and now she's making up for lost time. My friends are all jealous of the support she constantly provides me, as well as both of my sisters.

I frequently tell people that Monday is my favorite night of the week. My parents pick Moriah up from school and give me the afternoon to write. Then I join them for a cocktail and dinner. It's about the most relaxed I get. When the time comes to do something nice for Nana on her birthday in November, we like to make it something special. This year we all joined her for church, which made her very happy, then we gathered at Sallie's house for a great big Fall-ish brunch complete with precious children climbing all over her. Nothing could have made her happier.

The Menu

Soused French Toast with Cinnamon

———

Fast Apples

———

Cornmeal Coated Onion Rings

———

Brown Sugar Bacon

Soused French Toast with Cinnamon

This is a good dish for a bit of a crowd. Soaking the bread overnight makes for a very rich toast that's baked, not fried. Plus it saves you a step in the morning. The bourbon gives it a bit of a kick.

SERVES 6

1¼ cups milk
½ cup bourbon
9 eggs
¼ cup firmly packed light brown sugar
1 teaspoon ground cinnamon
12 thick slices salt rising bread, or other good white loaf

In a bowl beat together the milk and eggs. Mix in the sugar and cinnamon. Soak the bread slices in the batter on both sides, then place in a baking dish in which they fit tightly. You may stack the bread in a double layer. If any batter remains in the bowl, pour it over the bread. Cover the bread with plastic wrap and refrigerate at least 2 hours or overnight.

Preheat the oven to 400°. Lift the bread slices from the pan, shaking off excess batter. Place on a baking sheet and bake until golden and cooked through, turning once, about 12 minutes total. Serve immediately.

Fast Apples

Direct flavor in an easy dish. Good with chicken or pork for supper, as well.

SERVES 6

4 nice tart apples
2 tablespoons butter
   Juice and zest from 1 lemon
2 tablespoons honey

Peel, core, and slice the apples thinly. Heat the butter in the skillet and add the apples. Toss to coat. add the lemon juice and honey. Toss to coat and cook about 5 minutes, just to soften and allow the flavors to expand. Remove from the heat and serve warm. Garnish with the lemon zest.

Brown Sugar Bacon

This is fairly sinful. More like taking fairly sinful and adding a little more sin. But so tasty, too!

SERVES 6

12 slices bacon

3 tablespoons brown sugar

Preheat the oven to 350°. Place the bacon on the top section of a broiling pan and sprinkle the brown sugar over. Bake about 10 to 15 minutes until the bacon is crispy. Drain on paper towels and serve hot.

Cornmeal Onion Rings

The crispiest onion rings I've ever had. I could eat them every day.

SERVES 6

1	*12-ounce can beer*
2	*large eggs, beaten*
½	*cup buttermilk*
2½	*cups all-purpose flour*
2	*onions, cut in ½-inch rings*
1	*cup cornmeal*
4	*cups peanut or vegetable oil*

Combine the beer, eggs, buttermilk and 1½ cups flour in a mixing bowl. Pour the remaining flour into another bowl. Mix the cornmeal with the salt and pepper in another bowl. Dredge the onion rings in the flour, dip in the batter, then dredge in the cornmeal. Place on a plate and refrigerate for thirty minutes.

Heat the oil in a heavy saucepan to 350°. Remove the onion rings from the refrigerator and fry in handfuls for about 4 to 5 minutes until crisp and golden. Drain on paper and serve immediately with ketchup, hot sauce, or Hot Green Mustard Mayonnaise (p. 80).

13.

Saturday Night Steak

When I was a little girl, Saturday night was steak and martini night for Mama and Daddy, and Vienna sausage night for us. It worked for me. I loved digging the sausages out of the can with my fingers, and I loved watching the grown ups dancing to the Herb Alpert and the Tiujuana Brass records that Daddy so loved. Uncle Walton and Aunt Helen, Uncle Bob and Aunt Sue frequently made the scene. Aunt Helen had red fingernails and plastic cherries on her purse, both of which earned my constant fascination and utter admiration.

Being a grown up now myself, I have come to see the logic, nay the divine hand, which is inherent in an occasional Saturday Night Steak. I do not feed Moriah Vienna sausages, but she has had a turkey dog or two. She does not complain. I have asked Daddy for his Herb Alpert records, but he's not letting go. Saturday night is still steak night for them, too.

The Menu

Pan Seared Beef Strip with Jack Daniels Sauce

———

Leek and Potato Cakes

———

Roasted Acorn Squash

———

Sautéed Spinach with Lemon and Fennel

———

Poached Pears in Port Wine Sauce

Pan Seared Beef Strip with Jack Daniels Sauce

I don't eat a lot of beef, and when I do, I want it to be really good. At my market, they cut prime steaks to order. Always have them leave about a half inch of the fat. It really flavors the meat as it cooks.

SERVES 6

6	strip steaks cut about 1½-inch thick
	Olive oil
	Salt and freshly cracked black pepper
1	shallot, minced
½	cup Jack Daniels
1	cup cream
1	tablespoon chopped fresh parsley

Rinse the steaks and pat dry. Rub with a little olive and salt and pepper to taste. Heat a heavy frying pan with just a glaze of olive oil in it. When the pan is quite hot, add the steaks. Cook until the bottoms are nicely browned, then turn. When you turn the steaks, sprinkle in the shallot around the steaks. Cook the steaks a little under the desired doneness. Remove from the pan and keep warm. Deglaze the pan with the Jack Daniels. Careful, it may ignite. Don't panic, it will burn itself out quickly. When the bourbon is reduced to a glaze, add the cream, bring it to a boil, turn the heat down a bit and cook until it reaches sauce consistency. Season with salt and pepper. Plate the steaks and pour the sauce over.

Leek and Potato Cakes

I think the secret to making these is squeezing out as much of the water as you can. Be sure to use baking potatoes. Their high starch content holds the pancakes together. These are beautiful and addictively tasty.

SERVES 6

	Approximately 2 baking potatoes, scrubbed clean
1	*leek, white and barely green part, only*
2	*eggs, beaten*
2	*tablespoons all-purpose flour*
2½	*teaspoons salt*
	Black and white pepper to taste
½	*cup vegetable oil*

Coarsely grate the potatoes into a bowl, leaving the skin on. Cut the leek in half lengthwise and run both halves under the water, pulling back the layers to remove all the dirt. Shake dry, then cut in thin strips lengthwise. Gather together the potato and place in the center of a clean dish towel. Squeeze out as much moisture as possible. In a bowl mix the potatoes and leeks with the eggs, flour, salt, and pepper.

Heat half of the oil to just under smoking. Drop the potato mixture into the oil by spoonfuls. Use the spoon to spread the cakes out a bit to about ¼- to ½-inch thick. Cook about 3 to 5 minutes per side. Serve warm.

Roast Acorn Squash with Maple

A very pretty, simple, delicious side dish. It really completes the plate.

SERVES 6

1	acorn squash
	Salt and pepper to taste
3	tablespoons butter
½	cup maple syrup

Preheat the oven to 375°. Cut the squash in half and remove the seeds. Cut each half into ½-inch thick half circles. Cut away the peel. Season both sides with salt and pepper and place in a baking pan. Melt the butter and pour over the squash. Bake about 20 minutes until tender. Turn the squash over and pour over the maple syrup. Return to the oven and bake another 10 minutes until nicely browned and caramelized.

Sautéed Spinach with Lemon and Fennel

Goodness, I crave spinach. I love the baby spinach leaves which you can purchase already cleaned. The fennel and lemon work nicely together here.

SERVES 6

1	teaspoon fennel seeds
3	tablespoons olive oil
2	pounds spinach, cleaned
2	cloves garlic, chopped
	Salt and pepper to taste
	Juice and zest from 2 lemons

Heat a small skillet and toast the seeds until they start to pop. Pour into a small bowl and set aside. Heat the olive oil and add the spinach. Sprinkle over the garlic, fennel, salt, and pepper. Toss or stir the pan until the spinach is wilted. Squeeze in the lemon juice and lightly stir. Serve garnished with the lemon zest.

Pumpkins for Pumpkin Soup with Mustard Greens

Pan Seared Beef Strip

Hearts of Romaine with Beets, Red Onions, and Creamy Blue Cheese Dressing

Spiced Duck Breast over Mixed Greens

Poached Pears in Port Wine Sauce

This is a very elegant dessert. Serve it in a beautiful sorbet glass.

SERVES 6

1	orange peel
4	cups port wine
1	cinnamon stick
6	pods cardamom
6	firm pears

Use a carrot peeler or paring knife to remove the orange peel without the white pith (it's bitter).

Bring the port to a boil in a broad saucepan with the orange peel, cinnamon, and cardamom, and cook about 5 minutes. Peel the pears, cut in half lengthwise and use a melon baller to remove the core. Turn the port to low and submerge the pear halves in the port. If they don't completely submerge, you may turn them halfway through the cooking time. Poach the pears until tender. The time will vary with the ripeness of the pears, but about 15 minutes. Remove from the heat and let the pears cool in the syrup. Once they are cool, remove the pears and strain the port into a saucepan. Bring to a boil and reduce by half. Serve the pears in sherbet glasses with a bit of the syrup spooned over.

14.

Sunday Night Stew

I remember reading "The Bear" while I was first year at The University of Virginia. It's William Faulkner's long short story centered around bear hunting in Mississippi in November. The whole, long story feels most uncomfortable, wet and dark and cold. While reading it in my dorm room, I was picturing, smelling and feeling my own home in November. The leaves are gone. The landscape is gray. It rains all the time. It gets dark just past four o'clock. And you have four long months to go.

Time to feed your spirits and your tummy with some sustenance. Nothing soothes my edges better than a thick, rich, savory stew. The whole house fills with its aroma and makes you glad to be at home. This is a hunters' stew, giving a nod to the opening of a very popular rabbit season at home. There's no bear season anymore.

The Menu

White Bean Spread with Toasts

———

Rabbit Stew

———

Buttermilk Grits Squares

———

Hearts of Romaine with Beets, Red Onions, and Creamy Blue Cheese Dressing

———

Sweet Potato Pudding

White Bean Spread with Toasts

"Pâté," "pesto," there are lots of words you could use to make this sound fancier than it is. Whatever you call it, this spread is fast, cheap, and loaded with flavor to take the edge off of a chilly night.

Makes about 1 quart

3	cups cooked white beans
2	to 3 cloves garlic, chopped
2	tablespoons olive oil
1	tablespoon fresh squeezed lemon juice
1	tablespoon chopped fresh parsley
	Salt and pepper to taste

Place everything in the bowl of a food processor fitted with a steel blade and process until smooth. Taste for seasoning. Serve in a bowl with crackers, toasts, or fresh cut vegetables.

Rabbit Stew

Yes, I know that rabbits are cute. I grew up having Peter Rabbit read to me, as well. But if you're going to eat meat, rabbits are also an economical, ecologically sound, nutritious and very, very tasty food source. Rabbit gets tough after the first stage of cooking. It should be done briefly, or for a long time. This stew utilizes the latter method to produce a delicious stew with very tender meat.

SERVES 4 TO 6

4	tablespoons vegetable oil
1	rabbit, de-boned and cut in 2-inch pieces
	Salt and pepper to taste
5	tablespoons all-purpose flour
1	yellow onion, diced
3	cloves garlic, chopped
1	rib celery, diced
1	carrot, peeled and cut in 1-inch pieces
1	medium white turnip, peeled and cut in 1-inch pieces
4	cups dark chicken, beef or veal stock
1	cup red wine
2	teaspoons fresh rosemary
1	tablespoon fresh chopped parsley
1	scallion, thinly sliced

Heat the oil in a deep skillet or heavy saucepan. Salt and pepper the rabbit. Dust the rabbit pieces with about 2 tablespoons of the flour and brown on all sides in the oil. Remove from the heat and set aside. Stir the remaining flour into the oil and stir. Adjust the heat to about medium so that you can gradually brown the flour without burning it. You're making a roux! The darker you can get it, the richer the stew will be. Brown the flour for several minutes to a good copper penny color. Add all of the vegetables to the roux and stir. Let it cook several minutes, then gradually pour in the stock and wine, stirring to avoid lumps. Bring the mixture to a boil and turn the heat back down to medium. Add the rabbit pieces to the pot, along with the rosemary and some additional salt and pepper. Let the stew cook until the rabbit is tender, about 1 hour.

Taste and adjust the seasonings. Serve over the Buttermilk Grits Squares (It's also nice over wide egg noodles or rice).

Buttermilk Grits Squares

The buttermilk makes this extra rich, with a nice little twang.

SERVES 4 TO 6

---

6   cups buttermilk
1   teaspoon salt
1½ cups grits (not quick cooking)
2   tablespoons olive oil

Bring the buttermilk to a boil in a heavy saucepan. Stir in the grits and salt. Cook, stirring occasionally, for about 10 or 15 minutes until quite thick. Remove the pan from the heat and pour the grits into a baking dish. The grits should stand no higher than 1 inch up the sides of the pan. Smooth the top with a rubber spatula. Let cool, cover with plastic wrap, and refrigerate several hours or overnight.

When ready to serve, preheat the oven to 400°. Cut the grits into 3-inch squares and use a spatula to lift the squares out of the pan and onto a work surface. Brush a little olive oil onto a cookie sheet. Place the squares onto the cookie sheet and brush them with olive oil. Bake the squares about 10 minutes until nicely browned and warmed through. Serve at once.

Hearts of Romaine with Beets, Red Onions, and Creamy Blue Cheese Dressing

A beautiful fall salad, with some intense flavors. I frequently see people throw away the yellowish, crisp heart of the Romaine, but, to me its the most delicate part.

SERVES 4 TO 8

2	heads Romaine
3	beets
½	red onion, cut in thin circles
½	cup walnuts, toasted

Rinse and trim the beets. Cook in boiling, salted water about 10 minutes until tender. Drain and let cool. Slip off the skin and dice the beets. Remove the outer leaves from the Romaine until you reach the inner, lighter green and yellowish leaves. You may use the outer leaves for another purpose. Trim the core and cut the hearts lengthwise in quarters, leaving the core end intact. Rinse these well and let drain. Put one or two of the hearts on each salad plate. Lay a few red onion pieces over each. Sprinkle the beets and walnuts over and drizzle with the Creamy Blue Cheese Dressing.

Creamy Blue Cheese Dressing

MAKES ABOUT 1 PINT

1   cup mayonnaise (*preferably homemade, definitely not low fat*)
½   cup buttermilk
1   clove garlic, chopped (*only if using store bought mayo*)
     Dash Worcestershire sauce
¼   teaspoon red pepper
4   ounces good blue cheese (*I like Maytag*)

Place everything but the cheese in a the bowl of a food processor fitted with a steel blade and process smooth. Add the blue cheese and pulse the processor until you reach a nice creamy consistency with a few lumps of cheese. Taste and adjust the seasoning. Will keep covered in the refrigerator for up to a week.

Sweet Potato Pudding

A dessert that takes you back a few years. Nothing fancy, but so comforting!

SERVES 6 TO 8

2	medium sweet potatoes
4	eggs, beaten
2½	cups buttermilk
4	tablespoons butter, melted
1½	cups firmly packed brown sugar
1½	cups all-purpose flour
1½	teaspoons baking powder
1½	teaspoons baking soda
1	teaspoon ground cinnamon
¼	teaspoon nutmeg
½	teaspoon salt

Preheat the oven to 400°. Grease a 3 quart baking dish. Bake the sweet potatoes until quite soft. Peel them and mash. Mix 1½ cups of mashed sweet potato with the beaten eggs. Stir in the buttermilk and melted butter. Stir the dry ingredients together and then into the sweet potato mixture. Pour this into the baking dish. Prepare a water bath by pouring hot water into a larger baking pan. When you place the pudding into the water bath, the water should reach halfway up the sides of the pan. Bake for 40 minutes until a toothpick inserted in the center comes out clean. Serve warm with lightly sweetened whipped cream.

15.

Fancy Dinner at Home

A Pre-holiday Celebration

Sometimes I really like to dress up, put on perfume, set a perfect table with starched white linens, put Chet Baker on the stereo, light the candles and have a few of my closest friends over for an elegant meal I've spent hours preparing. When I would not enjoy doing this would be any given day between Thanksgiving and Christmas. I admire people who give Christmas parties, and I aspire to one day be like them. But I just can't handle it. For probably the same reason that I send Valentine's cards instead of Christmas cards, I do my most formal entertaining a couple of weeks before Thanksgiving. Formal because you *have* to is usually a drag. Formal on a whim is sexy.

I don't really go to that much trouble. My favorite number for dinner is six. Any more than that and they start stumbling over Moriah's Brio blocks. For those six (including me) I try to provide extra pampering and extra details, prepare dishes that I don't do every day. This meal would be equally delicious if you were wearing blue jeans or pajamas, but sometimes, on special nights, you just do more.

The Menu

Creamy Onion Soup

———

Crispy Cornmeal Croutons

———

Spiced Duck Breast over Mixed Greens

———

Popcorn Rice Cakes

———

Chocolate Soufflé with Chocolate Bourbon Sauce

Creamy Onion Soup

A velvety way to start a meal.

MAKES ABOUT 2 QUARTS TO SERVE 6

4	tablespoons butter
5	medium yellow onions, thinly sliced
1	tablespoon fresh thyme leaves
2	tablespoons dry sherry
3	Yukon gold potatoes, peeled and sliced thin
3½	cups beef stock
2	teaspoons salt or to taste
½	teaspoon black pepper
½	teaspoon white pepper
1	teaspoon sherry or white wine vinegar
½	cup cream (optional)
2	teaspoons fresh chopped parsley

Melt the butter in a stock pot, and add the onions and thyme. Stir to coat, and cook on medium low for about 40 minutes or until the onions are luxuriously soft and caramelized.

Add the sherry, turn up the heat, and cook until most of the sherry has evaporated. Add the potatoes, stock, salt, and pepper. Bring to a boil, reduce the heat to simmer and cook for about 30 minutes.

Transfer to the bowl of a food processor fitted with metal blade and purée. Hold a towel over the top of the processor to avoid messes and nasty burns. Return the puréed soup to the pot. Add the vinegar and cream, if desired. Reheat to a simmer. Taste and adjust the seasoning. Garnish with parsley and croutons, and serve at once.

Crispy Cornmeal Croutons

These are crunchy and nice, great with green salads, too.

MAKES ENOUGH FOR 12 SERVINGS FOR SOUP OR SALAD

4   cups water
½   teaspoon salt
1   cup grits
1   tablespoon butter
2   teaspoons olive oil

Bring the water and salt to a boil. Stir in the grits. Reduce the heat to medium low and cook for about 15 to 20 minutes, stirring occasionally. Until the grits are thickened.

Turn out into a greased 8 x 8-inch baking pan or pie plate and let cool. Refrigerate until they are quite cold and set, at least a couple of hours or overnight.

Preheat the oven to 400°. Lightly grease a baking pan. Cut the grits into small squares or strips and use a spatula to lift them onto the baking sheet. Separate them and brush them with olive oil. Bake for about 10 minutes until browned and crispy. Sprinkle with additional salt and serve warm or room temperature with soups or salads. Once they have been baked, they should be eaten within the day. However, the boiled grits may sit in the refrigerator for up to two days, then cut and baked.

Spiced Duck Breast over Mixed Greens

The flavors of the marinade are subtle and slightly exotic. This makes a very elegant main course salad.

SERVES 6 TO 8

4	whole boneless duck breasts, skin on
3	tablespoons red wine vinegar
3	cloves garlic, minced or thinly sliced
3	tablespoons orange marmalade
3	cloves
2	pods cardamom
1	bay leaf, broken in half
1	tablespoon fresh rosemary leaves
1	teaspoon salt
½	teaspoon freshly ground black pepper
½	teaspoon red pepper flakes
4	tablespoons olive oil

FOR THE SALAD:

½	pound mixed salad greens (sold as such at most grocers)
½	cup toasted almond slices
3	scallions, sliced thinly

Wash the duck breasts and pat dry. Cut them in half and, using a good sharp knife, score the skin just down to but not piercing the flesh, in diagonal lines going one direction and then another, forming a diamond pattern. Set aside while you mix up the marinade. Place all of the remaining ingredients in a mixing bowl and stir well to combine. Set the breasts down in this, turning them to coat well. Marinate covered in the refrigerator for at least 2 hours or overnight.

Heat a large cast iron skillet. Remove the breasts from the marinade, allowing most of the marinade to drip off of the breasts back into the bowl. Place the breasts skin side down in the skillet. Adjust the heat so that the breasts will brown nicely without burning. Once the skin is browned, about 4 minutes, turn and brown the flesh side. For medium rare, the breasts should be cooked after 8 minutes. If you prefer the breasts more well done, finish cooking them in a preheated 350° oven for about 5 more minutes. Remove the breasts to a cutting board and slice in finger thick strips along the diagonal. Pour any juices from the cutting board back into the marinade. Pour the marinade into a saucepan and bring to a boil. Reduce the heat slightly and cook down the marinade for a minute or two. Place the greens in a serving bowl. Pour the hot marinade over the greens and toss. Divide the greens among dinner plates. Garnish with the strips of duck breast and the almonds and scallions. Serve at once with the Popcorn Rice Cakes.

Popcorn Rice Cakes

I serve these on the side of the plate with the salad. You can make them slightly ahead of time and keep them warm in the oven. They're very nice under simple stews, as well.

MAKES ABOUT TWELVE 3-INCH RICE CAKES

4	cups *Your Basic Popcorn Rice*, cooked (p. 54)
¼	cup grated onion
¼	cup grated carrot
2	tablespoons freshly chopped parsley
1	egg, beaten
¼	cup cream or milk
2	tablespoons fresh bread crumbs
½	teaspoon salt
½	teaspoon black pepper
	Pinch white pepper
4	tablespoons olive oil

Mix everything together except the oil. Heat half the oil in a non-stick skillet. Form the rice mixture into small, flat cakes with your hand and cook in the oil, a few at a time. If they start to break up, try refrigerating the mixture for 30 minutes, then fry them. Press down on the cakes with a spatula as they cook, flattening them. Cook about 3 minutes on both sides until browned and crispy and cooked through. Add oil as needed. Drain on paper and serve. If necessary, these may be reheated in the oven just prior to serving.

You may sprinkle with additional salt as they go out.

Chocolate Soufflé

To my mind, the epitome of Fancy Dessert. Don't be afraid, they're really not that hard. When your guests have almost finished their entrées, just get back in the kitchen, beat your egg whites, fold, pour, pop in the oven and slip back in your chair. No one will have missed you, and you will surely be a star twenty minutes later when your soufflé has risen. Bring it to the table immediately, for all to admire.

SERVES 6

8	ounces bittersweet chocolate
6	tablespoons butter
2	tablespoons bourbon
6	eggs, separated
¼	teaspoon cream of tartar
½	cup sugar

Prepare a 2-quart soufflé dish by generously rubbing the sides with softened butter and dusting evenly with granulated sugar. Tap out any loose sugar.

Preheat the oven to 400°. Heat water to simmering in the bottom of a double boiler. Place the chocolate, butter and bourbon in the top of the double boiler, over the simmering water. Stir until smooth. Remove from heat and cool about 10 minutes.

(You may prepare the soufflé up to this point before serving dinner. If the mixture becomes stiff, reheat slightly before continuing). Beat in the egg yolks. In a very clean mixing bowl beat the egg whites until foamy. Add the cream of tartar and beat to soft peaks. Gradually add the sugar and beat until stiff. Use a rubber spatula to fold one-third of the egg whites into the chocolate mixture. Now fold the mixture gently back into the remaining whites.

Spoon the mixture into the soufflé dish and bake about 20 minutes until risen and set. Serve immediately with Chocolate Bourbon Sauce (recipe follows) and lightly sweetened whipped cream.

Chocolate Bourbon Sauce

You may leave out the bourbon, if you like.

MAKES 1 CUP

½	cup half and half
1	tablespoon sugar
1	tablespoon unsalted butter
4	ounces bittersweet chocolate, chopped
1	tablespoon bourbon

Place the cream, sugar, and butter in a heavy saucepan and bring to a boil. Remove from the heat and stir in the chocolate. Whisk in the bourbon. Serve warm.

16.

Cajun Thanksgiving

I'm blessed with the friendship of Steve Scalise, executive chef at the Corner Market and all around food nut. For the last ten Thanksgivings, Steve has overseen the cooking of hundreds of turkeys, close to a thousand pounds of stuffing, and lord knows how many gallons of giblet gravy. He sometimes sneaks one of his Mama's cajun specialties onto the menu. His Mama is Mary Louise Breaux Scalise, the best cook, and according to Steve, best mama, in Mid Town New Orleans.

I've met Mrs. Scalise only a few times, but I feel like I know her (and Mr. Scalise and Benny and Fabian and Jolie) as well as I know my own family. For ten years, now, Steve has been bragging about them, and about their Thanksgiving feast. I couldn't include all of the feasting items, it would have been a whole book. Heck, they prepare macaroni two different ways. "For Dad," Steve explains. These aren't Mrs. Scalise's exact recipes. Just some things I've picked up from listening to Steve, spying on him in the kitchen, and asking a million questions. He's looked them over and said they were okay. But probably not as good as dinner with the Scalises, right Steve?

The Menu

Roast Turkey with Dirty Rice Stuffing

Oyster Dressing

Mirlitons Stuffed with Tasso and Crab

Baked Macaroni

Glazed Sweet Potatoes

Steamed Broccoli and Cauliflower with Lemon and Garlic Butter

---

Pumpkin Pie with Pecan Crust

Roast Turkey with Dirty Rice Stuffing

The centerpiece of the feast.

FIGURE 1 POUND OF TURKEY PER PERSON

---

1   **turkey**
    Melted butter
    Salt and pepper

Fill the cavity of the bird with the stuffing. Truss the bird at the ankles. Place the turkey on the top section of a roasting pan. Brush all over with melted butter. Sprinkle generously with salt and pepper. Roast the turkey breast side up, basting every 30 minutes, for 12 to 15 minutes per pound. Let the turkey rest out of the oven for at least 20 minutes before carving.

Dirty Rice Stuffing

Steve and I used to stuff Cornish Hens with this, back in the early days of The Corner Market.

MAKES ABOUT 12 SERVINGS

	Turkey giblets and neck
	Turkey giblets and neck
3	tablespoons olive oil
1	yellow onion, diced
1	green bell pepper, diced
2	ribs celery, diced
3	cloves garlic, chopped
	Black pepper
	White pepper
	Cayenne
9	cup cooked rice, preferably popcorn
2	tablespoons chopped fresh parsley
3	scallions, thinly sliced

Rinse the neck bone and the gizzards. Place in a pot of water along with the trimmings from the onion, bell pepper, and celery, and some salt and pepper. Bring to a boil and simmer for about 20 minutes until the meat is cooked and tender. Remove the neck and giblets from the water and let cool. Dice the giblets and pull the meat from the neck. Set aside.

Heat the olive oil in a large skillet and cook the onion on medium high for about 4 minutes. Add the bell pepper, celery, garlic, salt, and pepper, and cook about 5 more minutes. Stir in the rice, the giblets and neck meat, the parsley and scallions. Taste and adjust the seasoning. If it seems a bit dry, you could moisten it with a bit of the cooking liquid from the giblets. Stuff the rice into the turkey and cook, or alternatively, serve the stuffing right away or put in a baking dish to reheat.

ture into the mirliton shells and sprinkle each with a bit of the bread crumbs. Bake about 30 minutes until slightly browned and heated through.

Glazed Sweet Potatoes

My most precious friend, John Perrin, grew up in the real Cajun country, in the midst of the bayou. Here, John tells me that the sweet potatoes grow faster than the dandelions. I'm always quizzing my friends about the food they grew up with. I asked John about sweet potatoes this year in the midst of his father's passing. His eyes shone (John's eyes always shine) as he talked about harvesting sweet 'taters with his Da. He talked about climbing up on piles of the tubers as high as a mountain in a child's vision.

John's Da was fading before I met him, but John's love and the stories about him live through every vibrant cell that is John. I hope this recipe passes a bit of that on, as well.

SERVES ABOUT 12

8	*sweet potatoes, scrubbed*
	Salt and black and red pepper to taste
1	*cup maple syrup*
4	*tablespoons butter, melted*
1	*cup cider, heated*

Preheat the oven to 300°. Grease a 3-quart casserole. Cut the sweet potatoes in quarters, lengthwise. Place in one layer cut side up in the casserole. Mix together the syrup, melted butter, and heated cider. Pour over the sweet potatoes. Bake uncovered about 30 minutes until quite tender and nicely glazed. Serve warm.

Baked Macaroni

A nice crispy top, but creamy throughout.

SERVES 8

1	pound large shell macaroni
2	teaspoons salt
1	tablespoon vegetable oil
4	tablespoons butter
½	yellow onion, diced small
4	tablespoons all-purpose flour
1	quart milk
5	cups grated cheese
	Salt and pepper to taste
½	cup fresh bread crumbs
	Paprika
3	tablespoons chopped fresh parsley

Butter a 3-quart baking dish. Bring a large pot of water to a rolling boil with the salt and vegetable oil. Stir in the noodles, bring back to a boil, and cook about 6 minutes until just done. Drain, cool, and place in a large mixing bowl. Toss with the oil and set aside.

Melt the butter in a saucepan. Add the onion and cook for about 2 minutes. Stir in the flour and cook about 4 minutes. Stir in the milk. Bring to a boil, reduce the heat to simmer, and cook about 15 minutes. Stir in half of the cheese. Pour the sauce over the noodles and mix well. Turn half the noodles into the baking dish, sprinkle with half of the remaining cheese, top with the rest of the noodles, then the cheese. Sprinkle the bread crumbs and parsley on top and give it a dash or two of paprika. Bake about 30 minutes until lightly browned and bubbly.

Steamed Broccoli and Cauliflower with Lemon and Garlic Butter

Steve insists on getting 2 cauliflower because he eats a whole one himself. This shouldn't be an issue in most households.

SERVES ABOUT 12

1	head broccoli
1	head cauliflower
6	tablespoons butter
3	cloves garlic, chopped
	Juice and zest from 2 lemons
1	tablespoon chopped fresh parsley

Rinse and trim the vegetables. Steam about 10 minutes with salted water until tender. Keep warm. Melt the butter in a saucepan. Add the garlic and cook just a minute—do not brown. Squeeze in the lemon. Remove from the heat and stir in the parsley and lemon zest. Place the vegetables on a serving platter and pour the sauce over. Serve warm.

Pumpkin Pie with Pecan Crust

The crust is divine, almost like a cookie.

SERVES 6

FOR THE PASTRY:

2 ½	cups all-purpose flour
2	teaspoons sugar
1	teaspoon salt
½	cup ground pecans
	Grated zest from 1 orange
½	cup shortening
½	cup cold butter, cut into bits
6	or 7 tablespoons ice water

FOR THE FILLING:

1½	cups cooked pumkin (strained, if using fresh)
⅔	cup firmly packed brown sugar
1	teaspoon ground cinnamon
½	teaspoon ground ginger
½	teaspoon salt
2	eggs, beaten
1½	cups milk
½	cup heavy cream

Stir together the flour, sugar, salt, nuts, and orange zest. Work the shortening and but-
ter in with a pastry blender or your fingertips until the mixture resembles coarse meal.
Sprinkle the water over the mixture. Work in quickly, until you have a ragged dough.
Divide in half, and shape into a disc. Wrap in plastic and refrigerate for at least 1 hour

or for as much as three days. This recipe requires only half of the dough, the remainder may be frozen for up to 3 months to use for another pumpkin pie.

When ready to use, roll out the dough to about ¼- to ⅛-inch thickness. Use the rolling pin to pick up and transfer the dough into a greased pie pan. Crimp the edges and fill.

Preheat the oven to 300°. Mix together the pumpkin, brown sugar, cinnamon, ginger, salt, eggs, milk, and cream. Pour into the prepared pastry and bake for 1 hour. Serve with slightly sweetened whipped cream.

Index